Kentucky
BACK ROAD RESTAURANT
Recipes

MOUNTAIN PARKWAY

A Cookbook &
Restaurant Guide

ANITA MUSGROVE

Great American Publishers
www.GreatAmericanPublishers.com
TOLL-FREE 1-888-854-5954

Great American Publishers

171 Lone Pine Church Road • Lena, MS 39094
TOLL-FREE 1-888-854-5954 • www.GreatAmericanPublishers.com

ISBN 978-1-934817-17-9

by Anita Musgrove

Layout and design by Cyndi Clark

10 9 8 7 6 5 4 3 2 1

Every effort has been made to ensure the accuracy of the information provided in this book.
However, dates, times, and locations are subject to change.
Please call or visit websites for up-to-date information before traveling.

To purchase books in quantity for corporate use, incentives, or fundraising,
please call Great American Publishers at 888-854-5954.

Contents

Preface

Okay, let's crank it up and go again . . .
this time to Kentucky, the second state in our
STATE BACK ROAD RESTAURANTS COOKBOOK SERIES.

WESTERN REGION

Monument at Abraham Lincoln's Birthplace

When someone says Kentucky I immediately have pictures running through my mind of waterfalls, open pastures with beautiful horses grazing, trains traveling through the hills as well as forests and caves to explore. Also I will never forget Kentucky is the birthplace of Abraham Lincoln. I did forget once, way back in sixth grade, on a test given by my teacher, Ms. Inez Crain. Of course she boldly pointed out to the whole class that I was the only one that missed the answer. Oh well, you can't know everything, but I'll always remember that.

I do, however, know what I like. I like traveling back roads with no particular place to be and no certain time to be there. When traveling leads to hunger, I like finding a mom-and-pop place to eat—the ones that serve food that embraces your taste buds and leaves you wanting more. Walk in as a stranger and leave feeling like part of the family, that's what I like best.

Western Kentucky is home to **Miss Hoss' Sweet Shop** in Greenville, named after her late husband whose nickname was Hoss. His favorite dessert was ***Banana Pudding*** and you will find that recipe in our book. Miss Hoss will tell you how God has led her to this place in time. Don't forget to stop in Henderson and taste some of the best BBQ around at **Thomason's**. They have been doing BBQ for over fifty years the old-fashioned way, in a masonry pit in the middle of the restaurant. Then don't leave without visiting the three sisters at **Ms. Janey's House** in Sacramento where you will be treated to the finest dining that will leave you with a deep appreciation for fine china, sterling silverware, and crisp napkins.

Not to be out-done, Central Kentucky offers many exciting places to explore. One of Kentucky's oldest eateries in continuous operation, **Cottage Inn** opened in 1929 in Louisville and still serves up simple and affordable food. Ms. Zuky is a treasure. **Riley's Bakery** in Bowling Green is also a must stop. They have been baking from scratch for seventy plus years. Walk in and smell the wonders that only fresh baked goods can offer. They still use their own Mother's recipes. Don't forget the tea cookies—everyone's favorite.

In the Bluegrass region, you will enjoy eating at places like **News Café** in Gratz, where you will be greeted by Earl and Linda New. I do not know which is better the food or all the antiques. They also have a B&B, so pack up and stay the night so you can see it all. Tell them Anita said hi. Then there is **Candleberry's Tearoom Café** in Frankfort that is a must see. In this place, where elegance meets deliciousness, do not leave without eating *Michele's Ham Salad* and their incredible desserts. Everything is made fresh in house. **Our Best Restaurant** in Smithfield is a trucker's dream stop. They showcase the cornmeal and flour that was once produced there. Let Kay Way tell you about the long ago days when the mill was a way of life in the area.

While traveling the back roads in Eastern Kentucky, be sure to stop in Whitesburg and visit with Ms. Karen and the girls at **Golden Girls Parkway Restaurant**. Get some of her *Hard Cinnamon Candy* and other homemade candies and fudge. You will be amazed at what you find on her menu and on her walls where she displays works from local artists. On the way out, be sure to sign the guest book, and by all means, don't leave without a hug. Eastern Kentucky is home to the original Colonel Harland Sanders Café where the famous fried chicken got its start. Visiting here is like stepping back in time to the 1940's. Enjoy a delicious meal and see the artifacts and memorabilia from the early days of the KFC restaurant system. It's free and fascinating.

Every restaurant in our second book, *Kentucky Back Road Restaurant Recipes*, deserves special mention, but there just isn't room for that. So read the book and get to know the finest people and restaurants in the country . . . those that just happen to call Kentucky home.

None of this would have been possible without good people behind me, believing in me and giving words of encouragement. Sheila Simmons has provided an opportunity that comes only once in most lifetimes. I thank you, Sheila, my publisher (and, daughter too, by the way) for what you've done, all of your life, for me. Brooke Craig, thank you for giving me encouragement to continue when it seems I am stuck in a deep hole with nowhere else to go. Diane Rothery, you keep me on the straight and narrow; thank you.

Christy Kent always has my back and is my sounding board, Krista Griffin is always there with an encouraging word and her infectious laugh makes us all smile, Christy Campbell encourages me with "Yes, you can do this; I believe in you;" you all have my gratitude.

Cyndi Clark, I give a very special thank you for your amazing ability to make my books beautiful. Roger Simmons you are the best in all you do and make us all better; I thank you. And last, but not least, Ellin Simmons, thank you lifting me up in prayer.

Most importantly, I thank God for bringing me to this point in life where I am able to express my gratitude to our Creator. I certainly have been blessed by the opportunity to learn about Kentucky while producing this cookbook. Thank you, Kentucky, for sharing your food and your people—I have found them all outstanding without fail. And for the reader, thank you for your time. Always remember, support your local restaurants; after all, you may enter a stranger, but chances are, you will leave as part of the family.

Please enjoy your trip through Kentucky . . . I did.

Anita Musgrove

Anita Musgrove

Author,
STATE BACK ROAD RESTAURANTS COOKBOOK SERIES

9

Western REGION

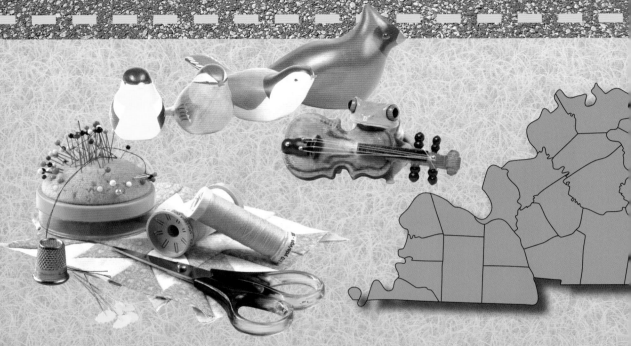

Beaver Dam Café

155 Spenser Lane
Beaver Dam, KY 42320
270-256-0988

The Beaver Dam Café has been a vital part of downtown Beaver Dam, Kentucky since the early 1920's. After five years closed, new owners have brought the Café back to its former role as a mainstay of downtown. The Café's old-fashioned home-style cooking and traditional diner fare has been updated with new flavors and recipes sure to become customer favorites. Come try a daily "plate lunch special" or choose from the regular menu items. Old-fashioned soda fountain favorites including hand-dipped ice cream and milkshakes are local favorites.

Sunday – Thursday:
6:00 am to 2:00 pm
Friday & Saturday:
6:00 am to 8:00 pm

Easy Shrimp & Grits

1 cup instant grits
Salt and pepper
½ stick butter
2 cups shredded sharp Cheddar cheese
1 pound shrimp, peeled and deveined
6 slices bacon, chopped
4 teaspoons fresh lemon juice
2 tablespoons fresh chopped parsley
1 cup thinly sliced green onions, optional
1 large clove garlic, minced

In medium saucepan, cook grits as instructed on box seasoning to taste with salt and pepper. Stir in butter and cheese. Keep covered until ready to serve. Rinse shrimp and pat dry. Fry bacon in a large skillet until browned and crisp; drain on a paper towel. Add shrimp to bacon grease in skillet along with lemon juice, parsley, green onions and garlic. Sauté over medium heat just until shrimp turn pink, about 3 minutes. Remove skillet from heat. Pour grits into a serving bowl. Pour shrimp mixture over grits. Garnish with crumbled bacon.

Restaurant Recipe

Blueberry Pie

Pastry for 2-crust pie

Scant (about ⅞) cup sugar

½ teaspoon mixed cardamom and cinnamon, a little more to taste but don't overdo

Pinch salt

1 teaspoon freshly squeezed lemon juice

2 tablespoons flour

2 tablespoons cornstarch

5 cups blueberries, picked over but not washed

2 tablespoons unsalted butter, melted

Preheat oven to 375°. Roll out 1 pastry crust into a circle of about 13 inches. Fit it into a pie plate, smoothing it along the bottom and leaving any overhang. Put in the refrigerator to cool.

Prepare filling by gently folding sugar, spices, salt, lemon juice, flour and cornstarch into berries using your hands. Add the melted butter and toss lightly with your hand. Remove pie pan from refrigerate. Scrape filling gently into pan, evening it out.

Roll remaining pastry crust out to 12 inches and, using your eye to judge or a ruler, cut it into 1-inch strips with a very sharp knife or pastry wheel. Weave a lattice over filling with strips. Trim bottom and top pastry strips as needed to within 1 inch of the rim of the pan. Turn both under together, and flute to

seal. You can use any left-over scraps to cut decorations.

Bake about 45 minutes, or until juices bubble up and crust is golden brown. If crust begins to darken too much before the pie is done, protect it with a pie protector or a few strips of foil loosely curved around the pan.

Cool completely before cutting. Serve with vanilla ice cream. Serves 6 to 8.

Restaurant Recipe

THINKSTOCK/ISTOCK/BELCHONOCKCOLLECTION

Cadiz Family Restaurant

324 Main Street
Cadiz, KY 42211
270-522-2249

Home to Cadiz Family Restaurant, the small town of Cadiz, Kentucky is a very close-knit town twenty miles west of Hopkinsville and sixty miles east of Paducah. The people of Cadiz are very friendly and kind. They are also very giving. With a population of only 14,000, more than $90,000 was raised during the Relay for Life event this year. Cadiz is also close to the Land Between the Lakes. Besides swimming, boating, and fishing the area features a Wranglers Camp, buffalo ranges, and lots of wildlife to observe. Everyone who visits Cadiz enjoys the town. The best place to eat when in the area is Cadiz Family Restaurant where you get great home-style cooking with friendly and efficient service.

Monday – Saturday: 5:00 am to 8:00 pm
Sunday: 6:00 am to 2:00 pm

Cadiz Family Restaurant Peach Pretzel Salad

This is one of the favorite items in our restaurant.

3 tablespoons sugar
¾ cup melted margarine
2 cups crushed pretzels

Mix together and press into a 9x13-inch pan. Bake at 350° for 15 minutes. Let cool.

1 (8-ounce) block cream cheese
1 (16-ounce) carton Cool Whip
½ cup sugar

Cream together the cream cheese, Cool Whip and sugar. Spread over the pretzel crust.

2 (3-ounce) boxes peach Jell-O
2½ cups boiling water

Dissolve Jell-O in boiling water. Chill until slightly thickened.

1 (28-ounce) can sliced peaches, drained

Place peach slices over the cream cheese mixture. Pour Jell-O mixture over the peaches. Chill before serving

Variation: Substitute fresh strawberries for peaches and use strawberry Jell-O.

Restaurant Recipe

Chocolate Pie

2 cups sugar

¼ cup self-rising flour

1 heaping tablespoon cocoa

3 egg yolks (reserve whites for meringue, if desired)

1 cup milk

1 tablespoon vanilla

1 (8-inch) pie shell, baked

Combine sugar, flour and cocoa; stir in egg yolks and milk. Microwave 5 minutes; stir. Microwave 2 minutes; stir. Mixture should be thick. If not, continue to microwave, 1 minute at a time, until thick. Stir in vanilla and pour into pie shell. Refrigerate, or top with meringue and bake.

Restaurant Recipe

The Farmhouse

220 State Route 81 North
Calhoun, KY 42327
270-273-3845

The Farmhouse, opened by Heath and Niki Frailley in 2012, is a country restaurant that provides guests with "Grandma's cooking." Their specialty and most popular dish is catfish, fried or grilled to mouth-watering perfection. The catfish is wild caught, not farmed, and arrives fresh daily from the Frailley Market. With great food made fresh daily and friendly, attentive service, you can't go wrong when you eat at The Farmhouse.

Wednesday & Thursday:
11:00 am to 7:30 pm
Friday & Saturday: 11:00 am to 8:30 pm
Sunday: 11:00 am to 3:00 pm

Log Cabin Café

1394 Highway 79
Dover, TN 37058
931-232-0220

Just over the Kentucky state line, you'll find Log Cabin Café in Dover, Tennessee—the best place to go for a good home-cooked meal. Caution: Once you make your first visit, you will surely be back for the amazing food, conscientious staff, and because it is an all-around friendly place. Local favorites include catfish, steak, shrimp, and hamburgers which are the best you can get for miles and miles around. You'll also enjoy the homemade potato chips, their outstanding Strawberry Shortcake and the Mozzarella Cheesesteak—sirloin steak strips cooked to perfection with mushrooms and onion and all topped with deliciously melted mozzarella cheese. Yum! Bring the family for a delicious meal that will please even the pickiest eaters, enjoy a night out with a special loved one, or just relax and have a cup of their excellent coffee. You can't go wrong at Log Cabin Café.

Our Famous Cabin Classic Burger

We take 2 thick 5 oz. burgers and smother them in BBQ sauce and grilled onions and mushrooms. Then we top it with lots of our delicious smoked bacon and tons of melted swiss and then put it all between two perfectly grilled Texas Toast.

Monday – Saturday:
6:00 am to 9:00 pm

Sunday:
6:00 am to 3:00 pm

THE WOOLDRIDGE MONUMENTS
Mayfield

The Wooldridge Monuments—often called "The Strange Procession That Never Moves"—is eighteen sandstone and Italian marble monuments. Colonel Henry G. Wooldridge commissioned the monuments to commemorate his family, pets, and himself.

A lifelong bachelor and very eccentric man, Wooldridge lost the last of his sisters in 1892 leaving him with no immediate family. The subject of many stories, one says the Minnie statue actually represents a childhood sweetheart whose early death prompted Wooldridge's bachelorhood. Another says that Wooldridge was such a miser that money was buried with him in his tomb.

The collection of life-sized statues, including a horse and two dogs named Tow Head and Bob, are all crammed into Henry's 17 by 33-foot plot in Maplewood Cemetery. All facing due east, the statues were carved and in place before Wooldridge died in May 1899 and have been featured in news stories as early as 1897 and on postcards since the 1920's.

Wooldridge included two statues of himself—one astride the horse name Fop and the other standing beside a lectern atop a pedestal. This second statue is carved in marble, supposedly in Italy. Despite what you may think when viewing so many monuments, Wooldridge is the only one entombed there. The lid of the above-ground marble vault is carved with a double-barrel shotgun.

Maplewood Cemetery
North 6th Street • Mayfield, KY 42066
270-254-6210

Coon Dog Inn Restaurant

512 Cassidy Avenue
Fredonia, KY 42411
270-545-3552

Nestled in the heart of the Fredonia Valley, Coon Dog Inn Restaurant is famous for country cooking created by owner Sharon Rodney and her staff. The restaurant originated from men gathering after the night's coon hunt to exchange stories and concoct meals of their prizes. The "coon dog" and hunting décor of the restaurant creates a rustic feel and aptly represents this heritage. Visitors often participate in the history of the town by shopping at Feagan's Furniture and continuing on to the Coon Dog Inn for breakfast, lunch or Friday night supper. Visit them on Facebook for daily specials, hours, and directions.

Monday – Saturday: 6:00 am to 2:00 pm
Sunday: 8:00 am to 2:00 pm
Friday Night: 4:00 pm to 8:00 pm

Cousin Karen's Carrot Cake

2 cups flour
2 cups sugar
2 teaspoons cinnamon
2 teaspoons baking soda
1 teaspoon salt
1½ cups Wesson oil
4 eggs, beaten
3 cups shredded carrots

Preheat oven to 350°. Spray 2 (9-inch) cake pans with nonstick spray for baking. Mix dry ingredients; add oil, eggs and carrots. Bake 35 minutes or until cake springs back when touched in the center (or a toothpick inserted in center comes out clean). Cool completely on rack.

Cream Cheese Frosting:

12 ounces cream cheese, softened
½ cup butter softened
1 (16-ounce) box powdered sugar
1 teaspoon vanilla
1 cup chopped walnuts

Cream together cream cheese and butter; slowly add powdered sugar and vanilla. When cake is completely cooled frost between layers then top and sides. Sprinkle chopped nuts over entire cake. Makes 12 servings.

Restaurant Recipe

Sharon's Cabbage Rolls

3 large heads cabbage
1½ cups uncooked rice
6 slices bacon, chopped
3 cups chopped onion
5 pounds ground beef
1 pound ground sausage
3 cloves garlic, minced
1 teaspoon salt
2 teaspoons pepper
½ teaspoon Cajun seasoning
4 eggs
6 prepared biscuits, crumbled

Sauce:

1 (106-ounce) can tomato sauce
1 (48-ounce) can tomato juice
1 (50-ounce) can cream of mushroom soup
2 cloves garlic, minced
Salt and pepper to taste

Core cabbage and boil, 1 head at a time, pulling whole leaves off as they come free. As they are loosened, remove leaves from water and set aside to cool. Continue with all 3 heads of cabbage until you have at least 30 large leaves. Devein cabbage leaves with sharp knife and set aside while preparing filling. Chop remaining cabbage and reserve.

Prepare rice using 3 cups water. Cook chopped bacon until done. Add onion, beef and sausage and cook until meat is cooked through. Drain grease and return meat to pot. Add garlic, salt, pepper and Cajun seasoning. Cool slightly; add cooked rice, eggs and crumbled biscuits. Cool.

While filling cooks, combine Sauce ingredients in a large bowl.

When filling is cool enough to handle, scoop ¼ cup onto each prepared cabbage leaf. Roll carefully, tucking in both sides. Spread chopped cabbage in bottom of 3 (9x12-inch) deep casserole dishes. Place rolls, seam side down, over cabbage. (You should be able to place about 10 rolls in each pan.)

Top generously with Sauce, cover and bake at 350° about 1 hour then reduce heat to 250° and cook an additional 2½ to 3 hours or until leaves are tender. Serve 1 or 2 rolls with your favorite sides and cornbread.

Restaurant Recipe

Jefferson Davis Pie

This is said to be a favorite pie enjoyed by Jefferson Davis and served with black coffee and a splash of Kentucky bourbon.

2 sticks butter, softened

1½ cups sugar

4 egg yolks

2 tablespoons flour

1 teaspoon cinnamon

1 teaspoon freshly grated nutmeg

½ teaspoon allspice

1 cup heavy cream

½ cup chopped dates

½ cup dark raisins

½ cup coarsely chopped pecans

1 (9-inch) pie shell, baked

Preheat oven to 300°. Cream the butter and sugar until light and fluffy. Beat in egg yolks. Add flour and spices and mix well. Add cream; mix well. Stir in dates, raisins and pecans. Pour into baked pie shell. Bake 40 minutes or until set (pie should jiggle only slightly in the very middle when shook). Prepare Meringue while pie bakes.

Meringue:

4 egg whites

½ cup sugar

Beat egg whites until foamy. Gradually add sugar and beat until stiff peaks form when you lift beaters. When pie is set, remove from oven and increase oven heat to 350°. Spread meringue over pie, mounding it up in the middle. Bake another 10 to 15 minutes or until golden brown. Cool to room temperature before cutting.

Variation: Top with Bourbon Whipped Cream instead of meringue.

Bourbon Whipped Cream:

1 cup heavy whipping cream

3 tablespoons sugar

1 tablespoon Kentucky bourbon

Whip cream, adding sugar gradually until stiff peaks form. Once cream is whipped, gently fold in the bourbon.

Local Favorite

JEFFERSON DAVIS MEMORIAL
Fairview

The Jefferson Davis Monument is a 351-foot concrete obelisk which is the focal point of Jefferson Davis State Historic Site—a Kentucky State Park commemorating the birthplace of Jefferson Davis, the first and only president of the Confederate States of America. The famous Kentuckian was born on this site on June 3, 1808.

First proposed in 1907, construction of the monument began in 1917 but stopped in 1918 due to rationing during World War I. Construction resumed in 1922 and finished in 1924 at a cost of $200,000. The monument is the tallest unreinforced concrete structure in the world. It is also the tallest concrete obelisk in the world; all of the taller obelisks are constructed with blocks of stone.

The monument is constructed on a foundation of solid Kentucky Limestone. The concrete walls are seven feet thick at the base, and taper to two feet thick at the top. At the top of the monument is an observation room with a window in each of the four walls. Originally, this room could only be reached by climbing stairs which went around the interior of the monument; an elevator, installed in 1929, now takes visitors to and from the observation room.

Open May 1st through October 31st, Jefferson Davis Historic Site covers 19 acres. At the visitors' center museum, you can watch a video describing Davis' life and the construction of the monument.

Jefferson Davis Historic Site
258 Pembroke-Fairview Road • Fairview, KY 42221
270-889-6100 • www.parks.ky.gov

Dockers Bayside Grille

Green Turtle Bay Resort
Grand Rivers, KY 42045
270-DOCKERS (270-362-5377)
www.greenturtlebay.com
facebook.com/greenturtlebay

Dockers Bayside Grille is the place to go for hearty or heart-healthy breakfast and lunch menu items. There are offerings that will be sure to please everyone in your group. Stop in after your morning exercise or swim for one of Dockers famous omelets. Or maybe you are just in the mood for yogurt and coffee. Dockers can fill your order. Lunch menu favorites include Dockers famous "Turtle Burger" or "Docker Dog," fresh-made salads, and homemade pies. On summer Sunday mornings, you might even find some fresh-made cinnamon buns, fragrant and hot from the oven. Dockers caters too. If you are bringing a group, please check with the resort's Group Sales and Events Coordinator for menu options and info on pricing. Dockers will be happy to put an entire meal or a tray of appetizers together for your group or event.

Seasonally, Monday – Friday:
7:00 am to 2:00 pm
Saturday & Sunday: 7:00 am to 3:00 pm

Dockers Coconut Cream Pie

1 cup sweetened flaked coconut

3 cups half-and-half

2 eggs, beaten

¾ cup sugar

½ cup all-purpose flour

¼ teaspoon salt

1 teaspoon vanilla extract

1 (9-inch) pie shell, baked

1 cup frozen whipped topping, thawed

Preheat oven to 350°. Spread coconut on a baking sheet and bake it, stirring occasionally, until golden brown, about 5 minutes. In a medium saucepan, combine half-and-half, eggs, sugar, flour and salt; mix well. Bring to a boil over low heat, stirring constantly. Remove pan from heat, and stir in ¾ cup of the toasted coconut and vanilla extract. Reserve remaining coconut to top the pie. Pour filling into pie shell and chill until firm, about 4 hours. Top with whipped topping and reserved coconut.

Restaurant Recipe

Dockers Meatloaf

Wednesday's plate lunch special

1½ pounds ground beef

1 egg

1 onion, chopped

1 cup milk

1 cup dried breadcrumbs
(or cracker crumbs)

Salt and pepper to taste

2 tablespoons brown sugar

2 tablespoons prepared mustard

⅓ cup ketchup

Preheat oven to 350°. In a large bowl, combine beef, egg, onion, milk and breadcrumbs. Season with salt and pepper to taste and place in a lightly greased 5x9-inch loaf pan, or form into a loaf and place in a lightly greased 9x13-inch baking dish. In a separate small bowl, combine brown sugar, mustard and ketchup. Mix well and pour over meatloaf. Bake 1 hour.

Restaurant Recipe

Miss Hoss' Sweet Shop

**135 South Main Street
Greenville, KY   42345
270-377-0290**

Miss Hoss' Sweet Shop specializes in all types of fudge, chocolates, cakes, pies, candy gift baskets, and many other sweets. They also have gourmet coffees and cappuccinos. Why is it called Miss Hoss' Sweet Shop? Linda's previous husband's nickname was Hoss (one of his favorite foods was banana pudding). They lived in the Kentucky Lake area and she was planning on opening a candy shop there. Hoss was killed in an accident before the shop became a reality. After moving back to her hometown of Greenville, God led Linda to open this shop.

SUMMER HOURS:
Monday – Thursday: 7:30 am to 6:00 pm
Friday: 7:30 am to 8:00 pm
Saturday: 9:00 am to 8:00 pm

WINTER HOURS:
Monday – Friday: 7:30 am to 6:00 pm
Saturday: 9:00 am to 5:00 pm

**Always open for events on the Square
till they end**

Banana Pudding

**1¼ cups sugar, divided
¼ cup flour
5 cups whole milk
4 eggs, separated
1 teaspoon salt
1 teaspoon vanilla
Vanilla wafers or graham crackers
5 to 6 ripe bananas**

Blend 1 cup sugar and flour together in a 4-quart pot. Add milk and whisk. Cook over medium-low heat stirring frequently to prevent sticking or scorching. Beat egg yolks in a 2 cup measure. Add a little hot milk to eggs to temper them; add back to milk mixture. Continue to cook, stirring constantly, until mixture is thick and bubbly. (It should coat a spoon; I prefer a wooden spoon.) Add salt and vanilla; stir well. In a 3- to 4-quart casserole dish, layer vanilla wafers, then a layer of about a third of the sliced bananas. Layer a third of the custard on top of this. Repeat 2 more times.

Prepare meringue using egg whites and about ¼ cup sugar. Beat until stiff peaks form. Spread over custard. Bake at 375° until meringue is golden brown, about 15 minutes. Serve warm. Refrigerate leftovers if there are any.

Restaurant Recipe

Apple Pecan Cake

½ cup chopped pecans

2 teaspoons ground cinnamon

1½ cups sugar, divided

½ cup butter, softened

1 teaspoon vanilla

2 eggs

2 cups sifted flour

1 teaspoon baking powder

1 teaspoon baking soda

½ teaspoon salt

1 cup sour cream

2 medium apples, pared
and thinly sliced

Preheat oven to 350°. Mix pecans, cinnamon and ½ cup sugar in a small bowl. In a separate bowl and using an electric mixer, cream butter; gradually add remaining 1 cup sugar. Mix until light and fluffy. Add vanilla then eggs, 1 at a time, beating well between additions. Sift flour, baking powder, baking soda and salt together; beat into butter mixture alternately with sour cream. Spread half of batter in greased 9-inch tube pan with removable bottom. Top with apple slices and ½ cup pecan mixture. Add remaining batter; top with remaining pecan mixture. Bake 40 minutes or until top springs back when pressed. Cool 30 minutes in pan; remove and cool completely before slicing.

Local Favorite

American Café

306 North Ewing Street
Guthrie, KY 42234
270-483-2288

If you are in the Guthrie area, don't miss American Café. You will enjoy great service from a friendly staff and terrific food. Visit for breakfast and enjoy a delicious sausage biscuit or breakfast made to order. American Café's lunch specials are a local favorite. Enjoy a different menu each day from pork cutlet with mushroom gravy to fried chicken to barbecue pork chops each served with a variety of sides including mashed potatoes, green peas, baked apples, pinto beans, fried squash, and more. Order from the menu for lunch or dinner— everyone loves their burgers. Whether you are a local or a visitor, you will be treated like family at American Café.

Monday – Saturday: 5:30 am to 8:00 pm
Sunday: 5:30 am to 2:00 pm

Blue and White Grill

318 Main Street • Hazel, KY 42049
270-492-8195
www.facebook.com/Blueandwhitegrill

Blue and White Grill, eight miles south of Murray, Kentucky on Highway 641, is owned and operated by John "Scooter" and Barb Paschall. Formerly known as Ann's Country Kitchen, it has been a staple in the community in some capacity since the 1950's. Serving breakfast, lunch, and dinner seven days a week, Blue and White features a menu that will please almost any appetite with pond-raised catfish dinners and plate lunches plus grilled shrimp, rib-eye steaks, chicken provolone, grilled pork chops, and homemade lasagna. Be sure to try their homemade pies—the best in the area. A newly remodeled dining area enhances the dining experience.

Voted Best Place to Eat Catfish by readers of *Murray Ledger and Times* for 2013.

Monday – Saturday: 6:00 am to 8:00 pm
Sunday: 6:00 am to 2:00 pm

Vinegar Slaw

10 pounds cabbage, chopped
1½ to 2 cups finely chopped onions
3 tablespoons salt
15 cups vinegar (1 gallon less 1 cup)
7 cups vegetable oil
(1 quart plus 3 cups)
Dash red pepper
1½ tablespoons minced garlic
3 tablespoons Dijon mustard
12 cups sugar
2 teaspoons pepper

Mix cabbage, onions and salt in a large bowl. Combine remaining ingredients in a large stockpot and bring to a boil. After boiling; remove from heat to cool. When cool, pour over cabbage mixture and mix well. This is a hit here in Hazel.

Restaurant Recipe

Buffalo Mac & Cheese

1 tablespoon butter

1 teaspoon minced garlic

1 cup cream

2 tablespoons buffalo sauce

Pinch salt

Pinch pepper

3 ounces (about ½ cup) cooked chicken

¼ cup shredded Cheddar cheese

¼ cup shredded provolone cheese

5 ounces cooked penne

1 tablespoon blue cheese crumbles

Melt butter in sauté pan. Add garlic, cream, buffalo sauce, salt, pepper and chicken; reduce. Add Cheddar and provolone cheeses. Stir constantly to keep cheeses from sticking. Add penne and toss until heated through. Garnish with blue cheese.

Restaurant Recipe

Commonwealth Kitchen & Bar

108 2nd Street
Henderson, KY 42420
270-212-2133
www.ckbhenderson.com

CKB is a gastropub serving simple food done well. It is not quite a bar and not quite a restaurant, but a unique combination of both. Visit and enjoy a full menu of CKB plates including salads, Wagyu beef burgers, and Kobe beef hot dogs. You are sure to enjoy the weekly specials. A local favorite are the Brussels sprouts, which are roasted to perfection and taste great. With its unique atmosphere and terrific food, you are guaranteed to love your visit to Commonwealth Kitchen & Bar.

Monday – Wednesday: 11:00 am to 9:00 pm

Thursday – Saturday: 11:00 am to 10:00 pm

Eastgate Family Restaurant

1648 2nd Street
Henderson, KY 42420
270-826-2654

Eastgate Family Restaurant is one of a few remaining places where you get delicious homemade comfort food. You will enjoy delicious dishes like chicken and dumplings, open-face roast beef, a salad bar with only fresh ingredients, chocolate pie, coconut pie, and other desserts made in-house daily the old-fashioned way. Their cabbage beef soup is a local favorite, and Eastgate's sweet tea and catfish are second to none. With an exceptional staff of long-term employees always ready to serve you, their motto is,

Cabbage Beef Soup

3 pounds ground beef
4 medium onions, chopped
4 medium bell peppers, chopped
4 medium onions, chopped
4 tablespoons sugar
4 tablespoons salt
3 tablespoons black pepper
½ cup Worcestershire sauce
1 (50-ounce) can beef consommé
1 (124-ounce) can kidney beans
1 (102-ounce) can crushed tomatoes
8 ounces tomato paste
2 gallons water
4 pounds cabbage, chopped

Brown ground beef with onions and bell peppers in a large soup pot; drain. Add remaining ingredients, except cabbage. Boil over medium heat about 30 minutes. Add cabbage and continue to cook about 20 minutes or just until cabbage is done. Cool completely then refrigerate 1 to 3 days; soup flavor is so much better the second or third day. Reheat before serving.

Restaurant Recipe

"Where friends and family come together." Owners Randy and Kim Duncan invite you to stop by and experience Eastgate Family Restaurant's hometown hospitality.

Monday – Saturday: 6:00 am to 8:00 pm

JOHN JAMES AUDUBON MUSEUM
Henderson

John James Audubon was the first artist or ornithologist to depict life-size birds and animals in their natural surroundings. Audubon lived in the town of Henderson because of its position on the Mississippi flyway, a bird migration route.

The museum's four exhibit halls chronicle Audubon's life, including his 1810-1819 residence in Henderson, housing one of the world's largest collections of original Audubon art that made the wildlife artist a legend. Highlights of the collection include the American Bald Eagle oil, a four-volume edition of the Birds of America, a personal seal, handwritten journals, and a silver service Audubon sent from England to his devoted wife Lucy. The personal artifacts and memorabilia portray the often difficult life of Audubon who was more starving artist than artistic success.

The museum building features small niches in its tower for nesting birds. It is just one of the highlights of the 700-acre John James Audubon Park which includes a gift shop, nature center, golf course, cottages, campground, manmade fishing lake, miles of hiking trails, and more.

3100 US Highway 41 North
Henderson, KY 42420
270-826-2247 • www.parks.ky.gov

Firedome Pizza & Wings

**2044 US 41
Henderson, KY 42420
270-831-1977**

Firedome Pizza & Wings features delicious wood-fired pizza with an amazing crust and the very best wings you will ever eat. The atmosphere is very unique as it is simply beautiful and also a cozy, makes-you-feel-at-home sports bar with plenty of televisions. The menu has a large selection of appetizers, all of which are extremely yummy, but the pizza and wings are the stars. The pizza has a perfect crust, flavorful sauce, fresh toppings, and plenty of cheese. The wings—particularly the char-grilled wings—have the perfect amount of heat and flavor. You won't get better wings in Kentucky; maybe the world. Whether you are visiting from out of town, stopping by with friends for a beer and to watch the game, or dining with family, Firedome Pizza & Wings is highly recommended.

**Tuesday – Friday: 4:00 pm to 9:00 pm
Saturday & Sunday: 11:00 am to 9:00 pm**

Kentucky Butter Cake

**3 cups all-purpose flour
2 cups sugar
1 teaspoon salt
1 teaspoon baking powder
½ teaspoon baking soda
1 cup buttermilk
1 cup butter, melted
2 teaspoons vanilla extract
4 eggs**

Preheat oven to 325°. In a large bowl, combine dry ingredients. Blend in buttermilk, butter and vanilla. Add eggs; beat 3 minutes at medium speed. Pour batter into a greased and floured Bundt pan. Bake 60 minutes, or until a wooden toothpick inserted into center of cake comes out clean. While cake is hot and still in the pan, poke holes in the top using a butter knife and pour Butter Sauce over the top. Let cake cool before removing from pan.

Butter Sauce:

**¾ cup sugar
⅓ cup butter
3 tablespoons water
2 teaspoons vanilla extract**

Combine all Butter Sauce ingredients in a small saucepan. Cook over medium heat until fully melted and combined (do not boil).

Local Favorite

Bacon and Tomato Vegetable Dip

1 cup sour cream

1 cup mayonnaise

2 large tomatoes, peeled and diced

4 slices bacon, cooked crisp and crumbled

1 teaspoon garlic powder

Combine ingredients in a serving bowl. Serve with fresh vegetables for dipping. This recipe is also delicious served with Wheat Thins or other light cracker for dipping. Another great use is to spread on a tortilla, top with your favorite deli meat and lettuce, roll and serve as a wrap. YUM!

Local Favorite

J & B Bar-B-Cue & Catering

48 South Holloway
Henderson, KY
Corner of Washington & Holloway
270-830-0033
www.jbbarbecue.com

J & B Bar-B-Cue & Catering is winner of "Best Barbecue in Henderson 2012" and is the home of the Open Pit Chicken. Their award-winning barbecue is some of the best you've ever eaten, from smoked half-chickens to ribs, pulled pork to mutton, they have it all. The delicious barbecue is served with an outstanding selection of sides—potato salad, coleslaw, baked beans, green beans, and French fries—as well as a number of beverages, including southern sweet tea. Not in the mood for barbeque? Not a problem. They offer hamburgers and cheeseburgers, pork chops, chicken tenders, and chef salad. A local favorite is the barbecue nachos. Finish off your delicious meal with banana pudding or a slice of homemade pie. Owners John Klein and Barry Burton pride themselves in the quality of their food and their superior service. Come see them soon.

Tuesday – Friday: 10:30 am to 6:00 pm
Saturday: 10:30 am to 1:00 pm

Lemonade

1 cup fresh-squeezed lemon juice

3 cups sugar

Water

In a gallon pitcher, add lemon juice, sugar and water to make a gallon. Mix well and refrigerate until ready to serve.

Restaurant Recipe

Thomason's Barbecue

701 Atkinson Street
Henderson, KY 42420
270-826-0654

Barbecue has been served at the corner of Atkinson and Lorb Streets for over fifty years. And Thomason's makes barbecue the old-fashioned way—cooked in a masonry pit in the middle of the restaurant. Ribs, pork, beef, mutton, chicken, ham, and turkey are cooked daily with hickory wood only. The dip is vinegar-based with lots of spices added. A local favorite is the BBQ Beans so be sure to try them when you stop at Thomason's Barbecue for the best barbecue around.

Tuesday – Friday: 10:00 am to 6:00 pm
Saturday: 10:00 am to 4:00 pm

Leigh's BBQ Potato Salad

10 pounds potatoes, boiled, peeled and chopped

4 eggs, boiled, peeled and chopped

8 ounces (about ½ cup) diced pimentos

8 ounces (about ½ cup) sweet relish

½ teaspoon salt

½ teaspoon pepper

½ teaspoon sugar

Pinch celery seed

Miracle Whip to taste

Mix all together with Miracle Whip until creamy (like mashed taters). Serve and enjoy.

Restaurant Recipe

Leigh's Barbecue

9405 Highway 60 West
Kevil, KY 42053
270-488-3434

In 1950, Leigh's Barbecue was started by Leonard Leigh. Eddie Leigh took over in 1971 continuing the great barbecue his father started. Now into their third generation, Ray Leigh II has joined Eddie to continue serving the same great pork shoulders that are smoked for twenty-four hours on an open pit, along with chicken and ribs. Smoked ham is available on Friday. Their delicious smoked meat is sliced in front of you and served hot. Be sure to try the homemade potato salad. Drop by for outstanding barbecue cooked the same way for sixty-four years.

Monday – Friday: 8:00 am to 3:30 pm

Breakfast Tortilla Roll Ups

2 cups hash brown potatoes

2 cups Egg Beaters or 8 eggs, beaten

6 tablespoons salsa

6 slices Broadbent's Pepper Bacon,
fried and crumbled (item 105 or P05)

6 large flour tortillas,
at room temperature

1 cup shredded Cheddar cheese
or to taste

Sour cream, optional

Spray skillet with cooking spray and place over medium heat. Add hash browns and cook until they start browning. Combine eggs and salsa in a bowl; pour into skillet with hash browns. Stir until thoroughly cooked. Add crumbled Broadbent's Pepper Bacon. Spoon into flour tortillas and top with cheese. Roll up and serve. Top with sour cream, if desired.

Restaurant Recipe

Broadbent's Gourmet Market & Deli

257 Mary Blue Road
Kuttawa, KY 42055
270-388-0609
www.broadbenthams.com

A unique place to visit and a delicious change of pace for your taste buds, Broadbent's has been dry curing country ham, bacon, and sausage, from our family's smokehouse to your family's table since 1909. For your convenience, Broadbent's offers mail order and wholesale options providing customers across America with old-fashioned flavored products. Broadbent's Gourmet Market & Deli is filled with their cured products along with a unique blend of more "Kentucky Proud Products," from jams and canned veggies to ice cream. Broadbent's Deli features a wide variety of sandwiches topped with delicious Broadbent's Meats and Kenny's Farmhouse Cheeses.

Monday – Friday: 8:00 am to 4:00 pm
Saturday: 9:00 am to 4:00 pm

Broadbent's Country Ham with Raisin Sauce

1 (16- to 17-pound) Broadbent's uncooked country ham (item 1617)

1 (23½ x19-inch) oven cooking bag

1 tablespoon all-purpose flour

2 (12-ounce) cans cola soft drink

Place ham in a large container, cover with water, and let stand 24 hours. Drain. Scrub ham in warm water with a stiff brush and rinse well. Add flour to oven cooking bag; shake to coat bag. Place ham, fat side up, in oven bag. Place bag in a 2-inch-deep roasting pan. Pour cola over ham. Insert a meat thermometer into ham, making sure it does not touch fat or bone. Close bag with tie; cut 6 (½-inch) slits in top of bag. Cover with aluminum foil. Bake at 325° for 4 hours. Remove foil, and bake 1 more hour, or until meat thermometer registers 140°. Remove from oven and cool slightly. Slice ham and serve with Raisin Sauce.

Raisin Sauce:

2 cups raisins

1½ cups water

Pinch salt

2 cups sugar

1 tablespoon cornstarch

1 tablespoon grated orange rind

3 tablespoons fresh orange juice

½ cup chopped pecans

Bring raisins, water and salt to a boil in a medium saucepan; reduce heat and simmer 30 minutes. Add sugar, cornstarch, orange rind and orange juice to raisin mixture; mix well. Return to a boil, stirring constantly, for 1 minute. Remove from heat and stir in pecans. Serve hot over warm ham.

Family Favorite

Country Pork Sausage Gravy

8 ounces Grandma Broadbent's pork sausage (item 202)

¼ cup all-purpose flour

2⅓ cups milk

Salt and pepper to taste

Cook sausage in large skillet over medium heat stirring until it crumbles and is no longer pink. Remove and drain, reserving 1 tablespoon of drippings in skillet. Whisk flour into drippings until smooth; cook, whisking constantly, 1 minute. Gradually whisk in milk and cook, whisking constantly, 5 to 7 minutes until thick. Stir in sausage, salt and pepper to taste. Serve over buttermilk biscuits or grits.

Restaurant Recipe

The Cabin Deli

215 Vista Drive
Kuttawa, KY 42055
270-388-6440
www.facebook.com/
thecabindeliandtreasure

Nestled in the small town of Kuttawa, on the north end of Barkley and Kentucky Lakes, is a tiny jewel of a place found in a bait shop. The Cabin Deli boasts homemade sandwiches, breads, soups, and desserts and is located inside The Cabin Bait and Tackle Shop. Their eclectic choice of breads is sure to please every palate. The recipes are based on family favorites passed from grandmother to daughter to granddaughters with each putting their own spin on the dishes. The Deli's potato soup is sure to warm the hearts of fishermen, home folk, and tourists alike. Visit The Cabin Deli and let Diane and Rose cook you something special. We guarantee you will not leave hungry.

Monday – Saturday: 6:30 am to 2:00 pm

Rose's Potato Soup

10 pounds potatoes, peeled, diced and rinsed
¼ cup minced fresh garlic
¼ cup diced celery
¼ cup diced onion
6 to 8 slices ham, diced
1 stick unsalted butter
⅛ teaspoon red pepper flakes
1 tablespoon salt
1 teaspoon pepper
1 (10.75-ounce) can cream of mushroom soup
2 cups shredded cheese (Cheddar, Colby, Jack, provolone)
1 (16-ounce) block Velveeta cheese
1 quart heavy cream

Place potatoes in a large pan filled with water to 1 inch above potatoes. Boil until tender. Add garlic, celery, onion, ham, butter, red pepper, salt and pepper. Boil until thick, about 1 hour. Add soup and both cheeses and heat. Add heavy cream and cook until thick. Serve with crackers or warm bread for dipping. Also delicious served with a pimento cheese sandwich.

Restaurant Recipe

GERMAN POW MURALS
Morganfield

From 1943 to the end of World War II, about 4,000 German prisoners of war were kept at Camp Breckinridge at Morganfield. One POW was Daniel Mayer, a house painter and self-taught artist who had drawn, but never painted before he was captured. Mayer painted more than 100 scenes, drawn from memory and picture postcards, on plywood wall panels in barracks, the mess hall, and the NCO club. Today only the NCO club survives including a 20 by 30-foot mural depicting a baroque castle in central Germany with a lake and the castle grounds.

Though Mayer's cause of death is listed as pneumonia, some say he died of a broken heart, 8000 miles from home and missing his wife and daughter whom he left behind in Sudetenland.

More than fifty-five years after his death, Mayer's daughter was able to make the trip to view the painting. Until that moment, the sixty-five-year-old woman had never seen a painting by her father, who had gone to war when she was five years old.

The NCO club was preserved during a $1.3 million restoration and is now home to the James D. Veatch Camp Breckinridge Museum and Arts Center and the Union County Historical Society and Arts Council.

Camp Breckinridge Museum & Arts Center
1116 Village Square Road • Morganfield, KY 42437
270-389-4420 • www.breckinridge-arts.org

#9 Steakhouse

1002 North Main Street
Madisonville, KY 42431
270-824-1099
www.9steakhouse.com
www.facebook.com/9steakhouse

#9 Steakhouse is a family-owned restaurant located in the heart of Western Kentucky offering only the finest selection of steaks as well as local seafood favorites such as fresh scallops, oysters, and shrimp and grits. The Steakhouse is the place for locals and out of town visitors to enjoy a relaxing dinner with delicious food and wonderful, caring service. #9 Steakhouse supports area coal miners with décor and memorabilia throughout the restaurant as well as in .its name. The owners and staff take tremendous pride in what they do; everyone who steps into their home is welcomed as family.

Tuesday – Thursday: 11:00 am to 9:00 pm
Friday & Saturday: 11:00 am to 10:00 pm
Sunday: 11:00 am to 3:00 pm

Dill Vinaigrette

#9 Steakhouse House Dressing

8 ounces fresh dill
4 ounces fresh parsley
2 garlic cloves
½ medium yellow onion, chopped
¼ cup sugar
2 teaspoons salt
2 beef bouillon cubes or 2 tablespoons beef base
8 ounces water
4 ounces white vinegar
8 ounces olive oil

In a blender, combine all ingredients except olive oil. As you blend, slowly add olive oil in a small, steady stream. (Adding oil very slowly is the key to dressing not separating upon standing.) Once olive oil is combined, turn off blender. If separation occurs, shake or stir well before serving. Serve directly over salads or pair with salmon, scallops, and other seafood.

Restaurant Recipe

Sautéed Shrimp & Weisenberger Mill Grits

#9 Steakhouse Signature Recipe

Weisenberger Mill Grits:

1 quart milk

1 quart water

2 sticks (8 ounces) butter

2 cups Weisenberger Mills Grits

Combine milk, water and butter in a large saucepan. Bring to a boil and add grits. Reduce heat and simmer, stirring occasionally, approximately 25 minutes or until most liquid is absorbed.

Red Eye Gravy:

¼ medium yellow onion, chopped

3 whole garlic cloves, minced

½ tablespoon olive oil

10 ounces brewed black coffee (leftover coffee works great)

½ cup brown sugar

8 ounces beef broth

In a medium saucepan, sweat onions and garlic in olive oil until onions are translucent. Add coffee and brown sugar. Bring to a simmer and reduce by half. Add beef broth and reduce by half again. Strain, reserving liquid.

Shrimp & Grits:

2 ounces (4 tablespoons) olive oil

20 (21- to 25-count) tail-on peeled shrimp

Salt and pepper to taste

2 tablespoons unsalted butter, room temperature

4 to 5 ounces heavy cream

½ cup shredded country ham

Father's Country Ham Pork Cracklin's for garnish

Heat olive oil in a sauté pan. Once hot, add shrimp. Season with salt and pepper and cook 5 to 7 minutes or until done. Drain excess oil and add Red Eye Gravy to same pan. Bring to simmer then remove from heat. Add butter, stirring until butter is completely melted.

In a second sauté pan, heat half the heavy cream; add grits. Add more heavy cream as needed to make grits the desired texture. Add ham and mix thoroughly.

Pour grits into 4 to 5 separate serving dishes. Top with shrimp and gravy using 4 to 5 shrimp per serving. Garnish top with pork cracklin's.

Restaurant Recipe

Granny's Strawberry Cake

1 box white cake mix

1 (3-ounce) box strawberry Jell-O

1 cup oil

4 eggs, beaten

½ cup milk

1 cup fresh or frozen chopped strawberries, drained

1 teaspoon baking powder

Combine all ingredients in a large mixing bowl. Bake in 3 layers according to package directions. Cool before icing.

Icing:

1 stick margarine, softened

2 (16-ounce) boxes powdered sugar

½ cup fresh or frozen chopped strawberries, drained

Cream margarine and powdered sugar. Add strawberries and beat well. When cake is cool, frost between layers and outside of cake.

Restaurant Recipe

The Crowded House

26 West Center Street
Madisonville, KY 42431
270-825-1178
www.thecrowdedhouse.co

The Crowded House is the tri-state area's first gastropub where gourmet meals meet craft brews in a tavern atmosphere. The Green Dragon Tavern is a nod to history and The Crowded House Restaurant is a celebration of today. In the restaurant, you will enjoy certified Angus steaks, fresh seafood, a house-favorite pork rib-eye, bison burgers, delicious sandwiches, homemade cakes, Cheesecake Factory cheesecakes, and much more. The tavern touts a full bar with twelve delicious brews on tap and many more available in bottles along with live music (weekly lineups can always be viewed via Facebook). Reservations and carryout available.

Tuesday – Saturday: 10:30 am to 10:00 pm

Cantaloupe Sorbet

1 cup sugar

1 cup water

4 cups seeded and cubed cantaloupe

2 tablespoons lemon juice

In a small saucepan, bring sugar and water to boil and cook until sugar is dissolved. Pour into a small bowl and refrigerate until cooled. Process cantaloupe, lemon juice and sugar syrup—working in batches if necessary—until well blended and melon is completely puréed. Freeze in ice cream freezer per manufacturer's instructions then place in a freezer container and freeze 3 to 4 hours or until fully set. Instead of using ice cream freezer, you can place this in the freezer until fully set, removing to beat with an electric mixer every 2 hours or so. Makes 1 quart.

Local Favorite

Larry, Darrell & Darrell BBQ

1106 Cuba Road
Mayfield, KY 42066
270-251-0464

With a name like Larry, Darrell & Darrell BBQ, you might wonder what to expect when you visit the restaurant. We have the answer. You should expect outstanding, award-winning barbecue in a clean restaurant and great service. Because that's what you get when you walk through the door. Local favorites include the brisket sandwich, barbecued pork, and barbecued ham. Don't miss the ribs—they are cooked to perfection and melt in your mouth. Simply put, Larry, Darrell & Darrell BBQ has the best barbecue around. It's nothing fancy; just great food and outstanding barbecue.

Monday – Friday: 10:00 am to 5:30 pm
Saturday: 9:30 am to 4:00 pm

Wilma's Kountry Kitchen

113 North 12th Street
Mayfield, KY 42066
270-247-1515

Who would've thought a little brick house in the old West Mayfield Addition would eventually become a restaurant? Dating back to 1918, it remained a residence until 1923. This little ninety-six-year-old building has stories to tell. Cotton Riley traded a house in the 1950's for the building. Back then it was famous for its country fried steak breakfast, fried pies, and lots of bootlegging. The property has changed hands fifteen times up until 1988, but the menu hasn't changed since the 1950's. Specializing in home-style cooking, Wilma's is still famous for their home-made pies—chocolate, caramel, lemon ice box, chocolate peanut butter crunch, and caramel peanut butter crunch, as well as apple and peach fried pies. If you're craving a delicious home-cooked meal, where the girls call you "hun" and the pies make your mouth water, then come on down to Wilma's Kountry Kitchen.

Monday – Saturday: 6:00 am to 2:00 pm

Old-Fashion Caramel Pie

1¼ cups sugar, divided
¾ cup flour
1½ cups milk
3 egg yolks, whisked
2 tablespoons butter
1 (8-inch) pie shell, baked

Place ½ cup sugar in saucepan. Set aside. Mix remaining ¾ cup sugar and flour in a bowl. Add milk to double boiler and heat until warm. Add sugar and flour mixture. Stir well, removing all clumps. Add whisked egg yolks and butter. Cook, stirring mixture frequently with spoon until it stands independently. Remove from heat. Cook reserved sugar in saucepan over low heat. Once sugar begins to dissolve, stir continually until sugar caramelizes to a nice brown color. Immediately add to double boiler mixture and place back on heat. Stir continually until smooth. Pour into pre-baked pie shell. Chill before serving.

Restaurant Recipe

Bayou Shrimp

1 pound 31/40 shrimp, peeled deveined and tails removed

Seasoned flour

Oil for frying

1 cup mayonnaise

4 tablespoons Asian ginger

5 tablespoons sweet habanero

1½ tablespoons Sriracha chili sauce

Coat shrimp in seasoned flour and fry in hot oil until done. Combine remaining ingredients to make a sauce. Toss cooked shrimp in sauce. Excellent for salads, soft tacos, or an appetizer.

Restaurant Recipe

The Feed Mill Restaurant and Bar

**3541 US Highway 60 E
Morganfield, KY 42437
270-389-0047
www.feedmillrestaurant.com**

The Feed Mill Restaurant is a family-owned establishment with a taste to please everyone. They are well-known for authentic Cajun cooking including Gumbo and Shrimp Creole. Their famed western Kentucky pit BBQ includes ribs, pork, ham, mutton, and chicken. For the adventurous, they feature alligator, crawfish, frog legs, and many more specialty seafoods. There is something to satisfy young and old, including fried chicken, catfish, soups, salads, and only the best beef on the market—Certified Angus Beef.

**Monday – Thursday: 10:30 am to 9:00 pm
Friday & Saturday: 10:30 am to 10:00 pm**

Quick–n–Easy Coconut Pie

2½ cups sugar, divided

⅓ cup cornstarch

2½ cups milk

4 eggs, separated

1¼ cups flaked coconut, divided

1 (9-inch) deep-dish pie shell, cooked

Combine 2 cups sugar, cornstarch and milk. Add egg yolks; mix well. Microwave 3 minutes; stir. Microwave another 3 minutes. Stir in 1 cup coconut, pour into pie shell. Beat egg whites until foamy. Add remaining ½ cup sugar, and beat until stiff. Spread over pie sealing to edges. Top with remaining ¼ cup coconut. Bake at 350° until brown, about 45 to 50 minutes.

Restaurant Recipe

Deloris's Café Inc.

2123 Triplett Street
Owensboro, KY 42303
270-689-0997

If you are looking for a great place to eat in Owensboro, Kentucky, DELORIS'S CAFÉ is the place. With its unique, old-time café atmosphere, Deloris's is truly the place where hungry people meet to eat. The food is served in ample amounts and always served with a smile from the staff. With the laid back atmosphere, you can take your time to enjoy the delicious food and with the attentive service, you'll never run out of your beverage. Don't miss Deloris's Café where you are always welcomed as family.

Monday – Friday: 5:00 am to 2:00 pm
Saturday & Sunday: 6:00 am to 2:00 pm

Chicken–N–Noodle Casserole

3 to 4 cups cooked chicken, cubed

1 (32-ounce) bag frozen California Blend Vegetables, thawed

3 (10.5 ounce) cans cream of mushroom soup

2 cups sour cream

2 (8-ounce) bags egg noodles, cooked

3 cups shredded cheese

Combine chicken, vegetables, soup and sour cream in a large baking dish. Bake at 350° until veggies are tender, about 1 hour. Stir in noodles. Top with cheese and return to oven until cheese is melted.

Family Favorite

Old Hickory Pit Bar-B-Q

338 Washington Avenue
Owensboro, KY 42301
270-926-9000
www.oldhickorybar-b-q.com

Old Hickory BBQ is home of the 2012 "BBQ Pitmasters" Kentucky Champion, as seen on the Destination America Channel. Opened in 1918, Old Hickory is "where local folks bring visitors for Owensboro's Best BBQ." Since 1918, Old Hickory has upheld the values and quality of their food because they have focused on one thing: "To consistently produce first-rate barbecue, there can be neither shortcuts nor compromise." This dedication to the old methods shows when you enjoy their outstanding barbecue with its distinctive flavor. This same commitment to quality is applied to their sides and their service. Old Hickory has been rated all over the country as one of the best BBQ restaurants in the US. This is the place you have to visit.

Sunday – Thursday: 9:00 am to 9:00 pm
Friday & Saturday: 9:00 am to 10:00 pm

Pangea Café

1320 Carter Road
Owensboro, KY 42301
270-689-9824
www.pangeacompany.com

Chef Justin Crandall, CC, a graduate of the Florida Culinary Institute, started his culinary career as a private chef and completed a two year internship under Chef Auguste Carriero, CEC, CCE, CC, a former Executive Chef at the PGA National Resort. Chef Crandall has worked as a saucier at Biltmore Estates as well as opened The Café in Ames, Iowa.

He is now owner and chef of Pangea Café and Catering Restaurant in Owensboro with the goal of creatively combining flavors of the world and bringing them together for your dining pleasure. His passion for cooking and love of food makes for an experience that will surpass your highest expectations. Pangea Café & Catering: Taste the Difference.

Tuesday & Wednesday:
11:00 am to 3:00 pm
Thursday: 11:00 am to 9:00 pm
Friday: 11:00 am to 10:00 pm
Saturday: 4:00 pm to 10:00 pm

Potato–Horseradish Salmon Roulade

Stuffed with spinach and sun-dried tomatoes, accompanied by a Bleu Cheese Bacon Bechamel

Tempura Batter:

1 egg
4 cups ice water
4 cups all-purpose flour

Mix ingredients well.

Salmon:

4 (6-ounce) salmon fillets
1 pound spinach
3 ounces (⅓ cup) sun-dried tomatoes, chopped
½ cup white wine
2 cups Tempura Batter
3 potatoes, shredded*
4 ounces (½ cup) horseradish root, peeled and shredded*
1 gallon oil for frying

Prep salmon by removing skin and cutting into portions. *(Chef's Hint: To skin salmon, lay it skin side down on cutting board and, starting from tail and using a flexible knife, make an incision. Once knife has started and while keeping knife at an angle pointed down toward cutting board, pull up on tail allowing knife to do the work.)* Make a cut down middle of fillets (not all the way through). You want to open fillet as you would a book.

Heat a little oil in a sauté pan over medium heat. Add spinach and sun-dried tomatoes. Deglaze with ½ cup white wine. Cover and cook until spinach is wilted; season with salt and pepper. Refrigerate to cool completely. *(Chef's Hint: To deglaze means liquid is added to loosen and dissolve the brown bits and pan drippings at the bottom of the pan that form during cooking and basting. This pulls flavor out. Deglazing liquid is usually broth, a marinade, or wine.)*

Once spinach and sun-dried tomatoes are completely cooled, put on prepped salmon and roll, jelly-roll fashion, paying attention to keeping stuffing inside the roll. Keep roll as tight as possible. Coat with Tempura Batter.

Combine horseradish root and potatoes. Place a handful onto a small sheet pan. Place battered salmon on top. Press more of the potato mixture onto the top and sides of the battered salmon. Submerge fish into hot oil (350°) using a basket. Fry till golden brown, around 7 minutes.

(Chef's Hint: Use a probe thermometer to check that center of fish is at 130°. If fish is not at temperature, place into a 350° oven till finished.)

Season finished fillets with salt and pepper and serve on top of Bleu Cheese Bacon Bechamel sauce.

(Chef's Hint: To keep the shredded potato and horseradish fresh, store in water until ready to use.)

Bleu Cheese Bacon Bechamel:

1 teaspoon oil

1 cup chopped bacon

1 onion, chopped

1 ounce (2 tablespoons) roasted and chopped garlic

½ cup white wine

1 quart chicken stock

¾ cup roux

1 quart cream

1 cup bleu cheese

Heat 1 teaspoon oil in saucepan. Add bacon and cook until crisp. Remove from saucepan and reserve for later, leaving grease in pan. Add onion and sweat; add garlic. Deglaze pan with white wine and reduce till almost dry. Add chicken stock and bring to boil; skim fat off top. Add cold roux and blend mixture by hand until smooth. Bring to a boil and add cream. Add bleu cheese and blend. Finish by crumbling bacon and stirring into sauce.

Restaurant Recipe

Gold Rush Café

400 Broadway
Paducah, KY 42001
270-443-4422

Gold Rush Café is a fun little country diner with a focus on breakfast. You'll enjoy their unique breakfast items, such as Scotch eggs, chicken-fried bacon, and chimichangas. They even serve up eggs from time to time. Every Friday Gold Rush has a "waffle-off" on Facebook. People submit ideas and the waffle with the most likes is made that Saturday. The winner even gets their waffle for free. Gold Rush Café is an adventure—you never know what you will find there.

Tuesday – Saturday: 7:00 am to 9:00 pm
Sunday: 9:00 am to 2:00 pm

XL Yeast Biscuits

1 cup warm water
¼ cup dry yeast
1⅛ cup sugar, divided
28 cups self-rising flour
2 tablespoons salt
7 tablespoons baking powder
2 pounds butter
10 cups buttermilk
1 pound butter, melted

Mix water, yeast and ⅛ cup sugar in mixing bowl; set aside. In a separate bowl, combine remaining 1 cup sugar with flour, salt and baking powder; cut in butter. Carefully add to yeast mixture; add buttermilk. Mix until well combined. Cover with plastic wrap or a damp towel; place in a warm dry environment until double in size, about 1 hour.

Remove a third of the dough and place on a floured surface. Being careful not to overwork the dough, roll to about ½ inch thick. Use a biscuit cutter to cut biscuits. Repeat with remaining dough adding the trimmings back each time. Place biscuits on a greased sheet pan, leaving a little gap between each. Brush with butter. Place in a warm dry place to rise again. Bake at 400° in a convection oven for around 30 minutes. (Baking times will vary based on oven, biscuit size and spacing in pan.) Makes about 48 biscuits.

Restaurant Recipe

Orange Dreamsicle Cake

1 box orange cake mix plus ingredients to prepare per directions

1 (3-ounce) box orange gelatin

1 cup boiling water

1 (3.4-ounce) box vanilla instant pudding mix

1 cup cold milk

1 teaspoon vanilla extra

1 teaspoon orange extract

1 (8-ounce) carton Cool Whip

Bake cake according to package directions in a 9x13-inch baking dish. Combine gelatin and boiling water. While cake is warm, poke several holes in the cake—I use the end of a wooden spoon—and drizzle gelatin over top. Cool completely. Beat pudding mix and milk until thick. Add vanilla, orange extract and Cool Whip; spread on cake. Refrigerate cake at least 1 hour. I make it the day before because the longer it sits, the better it tastes.

Restaurant Recipe

Heavenly Cakes & More

2201 Broadway Street
Paducah, KY 42001
270-443-3002
Find us on Facebook

Heavenly Cakes & More is a locally owned and run bakery and café located in mid-town in The Ritz hotel building which was built in 1927 and recently renovated. The café and bakery offer a wide variety of baked goods, light sandwiches, and salads. Owner and chef Ms. English is known for baking the best strawberry cake as well as fondant cakes and cakes made to order. Call today to schedule a Princess Party or Tea Party. Do you need a wedding cake? Give them a call.

Monday – Friday: 8:00 am to 4:00 pm

Kountry Kastle

3415 Clarks River Road
Paducah, KY 42003
270-443-9978

If there were such a thing as an eight-star rating for a restaurant, Kountry Kastle would deserve it. Started seventy-five years ago by Lake and Audrey Edward, this unique restaurant still serves the best food around. Current owners Max and Mary Ann Edwards continue the tradition of serving the best "dawgs" ever. This is definitely "dawg heaven." Drop by and enjoy a full menu from barbecue on toast to rib-eye sandwiches with freshly sliced meat, plus dawgs any way you like them, tamales made in house, and a full Southwest menu. Everything at Kountry Kastle is sure to please.

Monday – Wednesday:
9:00 am to 10:00 pm
Thursday: 9:00 am to 11:00 pm
Friday & Saturday: 9:00 am to midnight

Chili Tamales

Mush (Tamale Dough):

⅔ cup lard or beef fat

2 cups plain cornmeal

Salt, black pepper, garlic salt and onion salt to taste

¼ cup chopped onions or to taste

Place lard in pan and melt. Add cornmeal to make a mush. Add remaining dough ingredients. Mixture should be the consistency to wrap around meat filling.

Filling:

1¼ pounds top round beef, 2-inch cubes

Salt, black pepper, garlic salt and onion salt to taste

½ cup chopped onion or to taste

1 to 2 tablespoons Frank's Red Hot Sauce or Peck's Red Hot Sauce or to taste

1 (8-ounce) package tamale papers or dried corn husks

In a pressure cooker, place beef with seasonings and onion. Bring to pressure then cook on medium high 30 minutes. After depressurizing, remove meat from cooker and chop. Add hot sauce. Knead it up real good. Spread mush over tamale papers in a half circle. Place meat mixture over mush, roll tamale paper over and tie ends of paper. Freeze or to cook them right away, place in steamer and cook until hot through, about 1 hour.

Restaurant Recipe

White Bean Soup

3½ cups dried Northern beans

2 medium potatoes, peeled and chopped

3 stalks celery, finely diced

3 large carrots, chopped

1 medium onion, chopped

1 ham hock

1 teaspoon black pepper

1 tablespoon salt

Soak beans overnight in water. Next day, rinse beans. Place in a 6-quart saucepan ¾ full of water. Add remaining ingredients and bring to a slow boil. Continue to cook at a slow boil for 3 hours, stirring occasionally. Before serving, remove ham hock, chop meat off ham hock and put meat back in pan with soup.

Restaurant Recipe

Norman McDonald's Country Drive-In

6161 Highway 54
Philpot, KY 42366
270-729-4272

Years ago a young man had a dream of building a restaurant with tasty food and excellent service. With the help of family and friends, forty-nine years later that dream is still going strong. In the small town of Philpot, Mr. Norman McDonald has built a reputation of having the best burgers in east Daviess County. Local favorites include their Friday night catfish dinners and great rib-eye dinners. They say, "In a day and time when mom-and-pop restaurants are closing daily, we have kept our doors open, all thanks to our employees' hard work and loyal customers."

Monday: 10:00 am to 3:00 pm
Tuesday – Thursday: 10:00 am to 7:00 pm
Friday: 10:00 am to 8:00 pm
Saturday: 10:00 am to 7:00 pm

The Catfish Dock

**2003 West Everly Brothers Boulevard
Powderly, KY 42367
270-338-0055**

Located in the little town of Powderly, The Catfish Dock specializes in USA farm-raised catfish. This family-style restaurant serves up catfish that is seasoned with a special blend of spices, breaded, then deep-fried to a golden brown. It is served with homemade creamy coleslaw and sweet, crisp, hushpuppies. Be sure to try a side of green pickled tomatoes and wash it all down with a glass of sweet tea. The Catfish Dock serves a variety of foods including ribs, chicken, steaks, and seafood.

**Monday – Thursday: 10:30 am to 8:00 pm
Saturday: 10:30 am to 9:00 pm
Sunday: 11:00 am to 3:00 pm**

Broiled Catfish Marinade

12 ounces (1½ cups) red wine vinegar

5 ounces (½ cup plus 2 tablespoons) lemon juice

2½ teaspoons thyme

3 heaping tablespoons granulated onion

8 ounces (1 cup) salad oil

2½ teaspoons black pepper

5 teaspoons paprika

12 ounces (1½ cups) water

3 teaspoons granulated garlic

1 cup brown sugar

Combine all ingredients and mix well. Store in the refrigerator. When ready to use, marinade catfish fillets overnight before cooking as preferred.

Restaurant Recipe

Kay's KITCHEN

KOUNTRY KOOKIN'

365-2709

Kay's Kitchen

501 North Jefferson Street
Princeton, KY 42445
270-365-2709

Don't miss Kay's Kitchen where you will always be greeted with smiles and friendly faces from Kay and her staff. Kay's is a family-friendly restaurant, just four blocks from the courthouse in Princeton. The day starts at 5:30 am at Kay's, which serves the finest breakfast in town, available any time of the day. For lunch, you will enjoy hot plate lunches with meat and vegetables—all prepared from Kay's own family recipes. Looking for a fresh and tasty burger? You will be overjoyed by the Famous Kay's Burger. At Kay's Kitchen they are truly there to please you, so visit soon and let them serve you.

Monday – Thursday: 5:30 am to 2:00 pm
Friday: 5:30 am to 7:00 pm
Saturday: 5:30 am to 11:00 pm

Mexican Cornbread

1 (8.25-ounce) can cream-style corn

1½ cups cornmeal

1 cup milk

⅔ cup oil

3 eggs, beaten

2 slices cheese, cubed

½ cup chopped ham

2 small mild peppers, minced

1 small onion, finely chopped

Mix all ingredients together. Bake in a greased pan at 400° for 1 hour.

Restaurant Recipe

Muddy Piggs

1240 US Highway 62 West
Princeton, KY 42445
270-365-0040 • www.muddypiggs.com
www.facebook.com/MuddyPiggsRestaurantCatering

Denise Nelson's long-time dream has been to sell great barbecue. Husband Rob shared the dream, and they have embarked on adding diversity to the restaurant scene in Princeton, Kentucky, with their establishment, Muddy Piggs Barbecue and Catering.

The restaurant features house-made sides, salad dressings, desserts, and the best smoked barbecue you have ever tasted. Breakfast is served all day and they offer lunch specials, and delivery to area factories. Muddy Piggs catering can be customized to fit any size gathering, from a work lunch to a wedding

and everything in between. You ate the rest, now devour the BEST. Visit Muddy Piggs.

Sunday – Thursday:
6:30 am to 9:00 pm

Friday & Saturday:
6:30 am to 10:00 pm

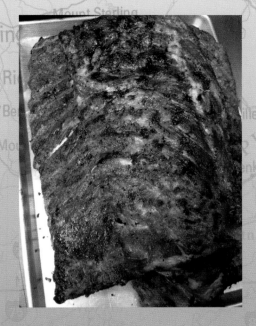

Coleslaw

Our family and patrons all love this coleslaw.

1 head cabbage
2 baby carrots
2 cups Miracle Whip
2 cups sugar

Shred cabbage and carrots in a food processor. Add Miracle Whip and sugar; mix well. Refrigerate at least 1 hour before serving.

Family Favorite &
Restaurant Recipe

Mama's Potato Salad

10 pounds potatoes
1 large onion, chopped
12 large eggs, boiled and chopped
¼ cup mustard
3 cups Miracle Whip
2 cups chopped sweet pickles
Salt and pepper to taste

Cube potatoes and cook in salted water until tender; drain. Combine with remaining ingredients while still hot. Mix well. Refrigerate until ready to serve.

Restaurant Recipe

Muddy Piggs Baked Beans

Our number one selling item.

2 (112-ounce) cans Showboat
pork and beans
2 cups chopped green bell peppers
2 cups chopped onions
2 (16-ounce) boxes brown sugar
2 cups ketchup
2 cups Muddy Piggs mild sauce

Mix all ingredients, pour into pans, cover and bake at 350° for 1 hour. Uncover and bake for an additional hour.

Restaurant Recipe

Pagliai's Italian Restaurant

**100 Micbeth Drive
Princeton, KY 42445
270-365-2323
www.pagliaisprinceton.com**

Serving Princeton and surrounding areas since 1989, Pagliai's offers something for everyone. The handmade pizza crusts can be ordered in a variety of thicknesses, including thin, double crust, and deep dish. Local favorites include the Deep Dish House and Meat Specials, loaded with cheese and fresh ingredients. These specialty pizzas weigh ten to twelve pounds each. Pagliai's is committed to providing guests with an upscale dining experience that is comfortable and delicious—and is unlike any other pizza place in Western Kentucky. They treat you like family—even inviting you to peek into their open kitchen to watch your favorite pizzas, pastas, sandwiches, and desserts being prepared. Enjoy a taste of tradition—visit Pagliai's in Princeton.

**Sunday – Thursday: 11:00 am to 9:30 pm
Friday & Saturday: 11:00 am to 10:00 pm**

Ham & Potato Pie

**3 potatoes, peeled and sliced
2 (9-inch) pie crusts
½ cup cubed cooked ham
½ cup shredded Cheddar cheese
4 to 5 eggs, beaten
Salt and pepper**

In a saucepan, boil potatoes in salted water about 15 minutes or until tender; drain. Arrange 1 pie crust in a 9-inch pie plate; set aside. When potatoes are drained well, spread into crust. Add ham and cheese. Season eggs with salt and pepper to taste. Pour into pie shell; cover with remaining crust. Pinch crusts together; vent top crust. Bake at 400° for 45 to 50 minutes, until golden. Serves 8.

Local Favorite

ADSMORE HOUSE & GARDENS
Princeton

Spread across a vast, four-acre estate, Adsmore House & Gardens, a circa 1854 Greek Revival home, is Kentucky's only living home museum. The name, Adsmore, is derived, as legend goes, from the numerous additions and remodeling projects that have taken place there over the years.

In addition to the house, which serves as the museum, the grounds include a 19th century carriage house that serves as a gift shop, and a rustic log cabin called Ratliff's Gun Shop—a completely functioning 1840's gunsmith business that tells the story of Princeton's first gunsmith, R. B. Ratliff.

When you see the wrought iron fences surrounding the grounds and view completely restored furnishings and buildings while touring with Victorian-costumed guides, you will feel like you have truly traveled back in time to visit the Victorian influences and lifestyles of the southern rich and famous.

304 N Jefferson St. • Princeton, KY 42445
270-365-3114

Roy's Bar-B-Q

101 Sara Lane
Russellville, KY 42276
270-726-8057
www.facebook.com/roys.barbq

Roy's Bar-B-Q was founded in 1983 by Ralph and Jolene Morgan who got their start serving barbecue and fishing bait from a trailer on a country road. This family-owned restaurant now sits on a hill in a new establishment which is decorated with memorabilia of the town's history and an array of UK and sports memorabilia. Roy's offers the best southern-style home cooking, daily plate lunches, catfish, barbecue, homemade pies, and much more. Now with three generations of family owners, they all contribute many hours and much dedication to make the restaurant a success. Many more family members help with cooking, serving, cashiering, and working the convenient drive-up window. Roy's also caters events of all types for members of the community and surrounding areas. Roy's Bar-B-Q has served the people of Logan County for more than thirty years and plans to be around for years to come.

Monday – Saturday: 10:00 am to 8:00 pm
Sunday: 10:00 am to 2:00 pm

Cheeseburger Casserole

This recipe is quick, easy to make, and guaranteed to be a family favorite. It helped me win my wife's heart years ago and now we enjoy it with our children at the dinner table.

1 pound hamburger meat
1 cup shredded hash browns
1 cup diced onion
1 teaspoon onion powder
1 teaspoon garlic powder
Salt and pepper to taste
2 (12-ounce) cans cream of mushroom soup
1 (16-ounce) bag frozen tater tots, cooked per package directions

Brown meat in a 12-inch sauté pan. When brown, add hash browns, onion, onion powder, garlic powder, and salt and pepper. Cook until hash browns are tender, stirring occasionally. Mix in soup and pour into a casserole dish. Layer the cooked tater tots over the top; set aside.

Cheese Sauce:

1 pound Velveeta Cheese, cubed
½ cup milk (plus more if needed to thin sauce)
¼ teaspoon crushed red pepper
2 tablespoons butter

Place ingredients in a microwave-safe bowl. Microwave on high, in 2 minute increments, whisking in between, until smooth and creamy. Drizzle over casserole, covering the entire dish.

Family Favorite

Boil chicken breasts in a pot of salted water for approximately 5 to 7 minutes or until an internal temperature reaches 165°. Drain chicken and cool in an ice bath. Once chicken is cool, hand pull into small chunks and place in a medium-size mixing bowl. Add pecans, cheese, lemon juice, onion, eggs and relish. Toss with a spoon to mix. Add salad dressing and mix gently until all ingredients are thoroughly combined. Add salt and pepper to taste.

Core just the green center out of tomatoes. With a knife, cut three quarters of the way down the tomato, repeat 3 more times in even intervals around the tomato so that tomato is cut in eighths. Place a lettuce leaf in a bowl and place the cut tomato on top. Stuff with chicken salad and garnish with a pickle. Ready to serve.

Restaurant Recipe

Chicken Salad Stuffed Tomato

This delicious chicken salad can be used many ways. Stuffed tomatoes are best when fresh, homegrown tomatoes can be found, but it's just as good on a sandwich or with crackers to cool you down on a hot and humid day.

4 (6-ounce) chicken breasts

1 cup roughly chopped pecans

½ cup shredded Cheddar cheese

Juice from 1 lemon

½ cup diced onion

2 hard-boiled eggs, sliced

½ cup sweet green relish

1¾ cups salad dressing

Salt and pepper

4 to 5 fresh red tomatoes

Iceberg lettuce leaves

Pickle for garnish

Mrs. Janey's House

530 Main Street
Sacramento, KY 42372
270-736-2821

Mrs. Janey's House in Sacramento, Kentucky, is owned and operated by three sisters who are retired teachers. Hospitality and delicious food have made Mrs. Janey's a popular gathering place for guests celebrating birthdays, anniversaries, reunions, and holidays, or to just enjoy their one-of-a-kind homemade meals. Diners at the tea house express appreciation for the fine china, sterling silverware, and crisp napkins in a room that reflects the season or holiday. The gift shop offers an opportunity to shop for unique gift items for yourself and others. You will enjoy the wide variety of gifts, antiques, and collectibles. Guests leave Mrs. Janey's House complimenting the homemade, delicious food and begging for the recipes. Friendships have been strengthened and some made at Mrs. Janey's House.

Tuesday: 10:00 am to 5:00 pm
Friday & Saturday: 10:00 am to 5:00 pm

Strawberry Scones

1 cup diced strawberries
⅓ cup plus 4 tablespoons sugar, divided
2½ cups self-rising flour
6 tablespoons unsalted butter, cut into pieces
1 cup heavy cream
1 large egg
1 tablespoon water

Preheat oven to 400°. Line a cookie sheet with parchment paper. In a small bowl, combine strawberries and 2 tablespoons sugar; set aside. In a large bowl, combine flour and ⅓ cup sugar. Use a pastry blender or fork to cut butter into flour until it resembles coarse crumbs. Stir in and toss strawberries until they are coated. Add cream and knead until mixture is combined. Dough will be sticky. Divide dough in 2 balls on lightly floured surface. Roll 1 dough ball into a 9-inch circle about ½ inch thick. Cut into 8 wedges. Repeat process for remaining dough. In a small, bowl beat together egg and water. Brush scones with egg mixture and sprinkle with remaining 2 tablespoons sugar. Place on cookie sheet. Bake 10 to 12 minutes or until golden brown. Serve with strawberry butter or Devonshire cream. Yields 16 scones.

Restaurant Recipe

Fresh Homemade Strawberry Cobbler

1 (1-pound) container fresh strawberries
1 cup sugar plus more for strawberries
1 stick butter
1 cup self-rising flour
1 cup milk

Rinse strawberries and slice. Place in a bowl, cover with sugar to taste and refrigerate at least 2 hours; overnight is best. Melt butter in an 8-inch square baking dish in oven set to 350°. While butter melts, combine sugar and flour in a mixing bowl and mix well. Add milk and mix until smooth. Pour batter over melted butter. Pour strawberries, with juice and sugar, over batter. Bake at 350° until golden brown, about 30 to 35 minutes.

Restaurant Recipe

Rissa's Place

7131 State Route 56 East
Sebree, KY 42455
270-835-2885
www.facebook.com/rissasplacesebree

Rissa's Place is the delicious result of years in the restaurant business by owner Clarissa Moseley who got her start in the 1980's working for "Moma Krina" at South Main Café. Years spent washing dishes, cooking, and waitressing provided the knowledge and expertise Clarissa needed to fulfill her dream of owning a restaurant. This dream became a reality in 1999 when she opened The Family Diner in the original location of South Main Café. Today, Rissa's Place serves great food with outstanding service that comes from Clarissa's years of experience and passion for the business.

Tuesday – Friday 7:00 am to 7:00 pm
Saturday: 7:00 am to 2:00 pm
Sunday: 10:00 am to 3:00 pm

Slab Town Food and Fuel

**11972 State Route 131
Symsonia, KY 42082
270-851-3319**

Nestled on the corner of the four-way stop in Symsonia you'll find the comfortable restaurant known for the unmistakable aroma it emits into the surrounding neighborhood. The smell is slow-cooked meat enticing people of the area to come. Once inside, the comforts of home are apparent and you'll find a vast assortment of dining choices. From the oven to the grill, Slab Town caters to your preferences. Regardless of the meal, the owners are available to turn any experience into a treat. Family-owned and operated, Slab Town is the one stop you won't want to skip.

**Monday – Saturday: 6:00 am to 7:30 pm
Sunday: 8:00 am to 6:00 pm**

Slab Town Club

**2 slices ham
2 slices turkey
Two slices white or wheat toast
1 slice American cheese
1 slice tomato
Mayonnaise to taste
2 pieces cooked bacon**

Gently grill ham and turkey. Top one slice of toast with both slices ham, cheese, tomato, mayonnaise, both pieces of bacon and then turkey. Add other slice of toast to finish the sandwich. Cut in fourths and run each cut through with a toothpick to keep everything in place.

Restaurant Recipe

HANDMADE BROOMS
Symsonia

You may think of brooms only as a functional necessity, but once you visit Henson Brooms & General Store, you'll think of brooms as an art form. Henson is famous for award winning, nationally known handmade brooms—more than twelve varieties. Henson handcrafted brooms have been featured on the television shows *Dr. Quinn, Medicine Woman* and *Martha Stewart Living*, and the ballet "Angels in the Architecture" performed by the Northern Ballet Theatre in Leeds, England, and the Broadway play, Disney's "Beauty and the Beast," as well as in many other television, theatre, and photography projects.

Henson Brooms & General Store is located at the village of Symsonia, just outside of Paducah in a building that is a replica of a 1930's era country store. There you will find high-quality handmade brooms at the area's only fourth-generation family broom making business plus many fine Amish products in their old general store. You can even view the Henson Homestead Cabin, circa 1930.

If you enjoy history, love the old slower pace of days gone by, or just want to escape your world for a few moments then you definitely want to plan at stop at Henson Brooms & General Store where they invite you to drop in, watch brooms being made, or take a stress reliever and just sit and talk by the fire.

Henson Brooms & General Store
1060 Kentucky 348
Symsonia, KY 42082
270-851-8510
www.hensonbrooms.com

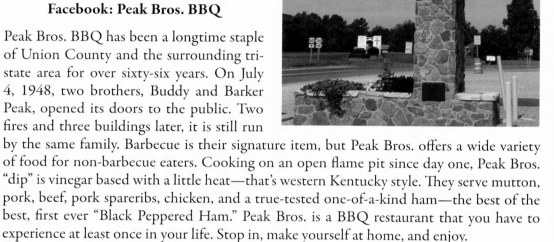

Peak Bros. BBQ

6353 US Highway 60 West
Waverly, KY 42462
270-389-0267
Facebook: Peak Bros. BBQ

Peak Bros. BBQ has been a longtime staple of Union County and the surrounding tri-state area for over sixty-six years. On July 4, 1948, two brothers, Buddy and Barker Peak, opened its doors to the public. Two fires and three buildings later, it is still run by the same family. Barbecue is their signature item, but Peak Bros. offers a wide variety of food for non-barbecue eaters. Cooking on an open flame pit since day one, Peak Bros. "dip" is vinegar based with a little heat—that's western Kentucky style. They serve mutton, pork, beef, pork spareribs, chicken, and a true-tested one-of-a-kind ham—the best of the best, first ever "Black Peppered Ham." Peak Bros. is a BBQ restaurant that you have to experience at least once in your life. Stop in, make yourself at home, and enjoy.

Tuesday & Wednesday:
10:00 am to 9:00 pm
Thursday: 10:00 am to 10:00 pm
Friday & Saturday: 8:00 am to 10:00 pm
Sunday: 8:00 am to 3:00 pm
Sunday Buffet: 11:00 am to 2:00 pm

Peak Bros. Fried Chicken

Served only on the Sunday buffet

1 whole chicken, cut for frying

1 tablespoon cayenne pepper

1 tablespoon seasoned salt

Put chicken pieces in a bowl with water to cover. Add spices to the water. Let sit in the refrigerator for at least 1 day.

Batter:

2 cups flour

Pinch salt

1 teaspoon cayenne pepper

Combine flour and spices in a large bowl. Put chicken in flour mixture and shake to coat well. Deep fry at 350° for 16 minutes. Remove from oil and serve.

Restaurant Recipe

BBQ Nachos

1 (16-ounce) bag nacho corn chips

½ cup prepared baked beans

½ to 1 cup BBQ meat (pulled, chopped, chipped in dip)

Chopped pickles to taste

Chopped onions to taste

Chopped jalapeños to taste

½ cup shredded or sliced cheese

Optional: shredded lettuce, chopped tomato or other vegetables

Start by crunching up enough chips to sit in the bottom of your plate or serving dish. Add a single layer of baked beans. Top with your favorite BBQ meat. (We use chipped ham. It's a little spicy and adds some heat to the nachos.) Sprinkle pickles, onions and jalapeños on top using however much you choose. Place cheese on top of all that yummy goodness and microwave it long enough to melt the cheese. Add corn chips all around your plate and serve with sour cream.

Restaurant Recipe

Kelly Rae's Country Café

10130 Highway 54
Whitesville, KY 42378
270-233-9100

For more than five years, Kelly Rae's Country Café has served home-cooked lunches and dinners. They serve breakfast and lunch seven days a week and catfish dinners on Friday evenings. As a small, family-run restaurant, the Kelly Rae's team focuses on serving delicious food with a smile and treating every customer like family. Located twelve miles east of Owensboro on Highway 54, come join them for lots of good food, good friends, and good times.

Monday – Saturday: 5:00 am to 2:00 pm
Friday: 4:00 pm to 8:00 pm
Sunday: 6:00 am to 2:00 pm

Meatloaf

1½ pounds ground beef
½ cup finely chopped onion
¾ cup breadcrumbs or crushed crackers or oatmeal
½ cup milk
1 teaspoon salt
2 tablespoons Worcestershire sauce
2 eggs, beaten
½ teaspoon pepper
¾ cup barbecue sauce
Ketchup

Using your hands, mix all ingredients except ketchup well. Shape into an oval loaf. Place in loaf pan (any baking pan with sides will work). Bake at 350° for 1 hour or until middle is no longer pink. During the last 15 minutes of baking, cover top with ketchup.

Restaurant Recipe

WORLD'S LARGEST SASSAFRAS TREE
Owensboro

The average sassafras tree is thirty to fifty feet tall. There are some around that are sixty feet tall, but the World's Largest Sassafras Tree is over one hundred feet tall. This amazing tree, located on one of Owensboro's main streets, is twenty-one feet in circumference and is approximately 300 years old.

As legend goes, the owner guarded the tree with a shotgun when threatened by bulldozers with the widening of a highway in 1957. She held them off at gunpoint until a call to the governor resulted in the tree's protection.

While in Owensboro, you may want to also check out the International Bluegrass Music Museum—the only international museum dedicated to preserving and showcasing the history, collections, and artifacts of bluegrass music. And don't miss the Western Kentucky Botanical Garden featuring ten established gardens—Butterfly, Rose, Daylily, Iris, Herb, Luettgen Ericaceous, Ornamental Grass, Fruit & Berry, and the Takahashi Japanese Memorial Garden as well as a Children's Garden.

World's Largest Sassafras Tree
2100 block of Frederica Street
Owensboro, KY 42301
www.visitowensboro.com

Stuffed Flounder

Stuffing:

2 tablespoons bacon drippings

1 medium onion, chopped

2 cloves garlic, crushed

2 tablespoons minced celery

2 tablespoons minced bell pepper

1 teaspoon salt

½ teaspoon pepper

⅛ teaspoon dried thyme

1 tablespoon dried parsley

1 egg

¾ cup breadcrumbs

1 cup crabmeat

Heat bacon drippings over medium heat. Add onion, garlic, celery and bell pepper; sauté until soft. Add remaining stuffing ingredients and mix well.

Flounder:

3 to 4 pound flounder, cleaned and filleted

Salt

Butter

Cut a big pocket in fish; season with salt to taste. Fill with stuffing. Melt butter in an oven-safe skillet. Add fish, dark side down. Cover and bake at 375° for 30 minutes. Uncover and bake an addition 5 to 10 minutes.

Local Favorite

Kentucky Spiced Lemonade

4 cups sugar

2 cups water

6 cinnamon sticks

3 cups lemon juice

In a saucepan over medium high heat, combine sugar, water and cinnamon. Bring to a boil, then reduce heat and simmer 10 minutes. Cool. In a large pitcher, combine spiced syrup with 2 gallons water and lemon juice. Mix well. Chill until ready to serve.

Local Favorite

THINKSTOCK/FUSE

Tomato–Basil Tortellini

2 teaspoons extra-virgin olive oil

1 medium onion, chopped

1 (14-ounce) can chopped tomatoes

Salt and freshly ground pepper

1 (12-ounce) package frozen cheese tortellini

¼ cup chopped fresh basil

¼ to ½ cup grated Parmesan cheese

Fill a stockpot two-thirds full with salted water and bring to a boil. In a large skillet, heat oil over medium-high heat. Brown onion in hot oil. Add tomatoes (with juice) and bring to a boil. Reduce heat to medium-low and simmer, stirring occasionally, until sauce is slightly thickened, about 10 minutes. Season with salt and pepper to taste. Add tortellini to boiling water and cook al dente, about 5 minutes. Drain and transfer to a large bowl. Toss with tomato sauce. Stir in basil. Serve topped with Parmesan cheese to taste.

Local Favorite

SHUTTERSTOCK.COM/LIV FRIIS-LARSEN

Turtle Cake

1 box German chocolate cake mix, plus ingredients to prepare

Butter

1 (11-ounce) bag caramel bits

½ cup evaporated milk

1 (6-ounce) package chocolate chips

1 cup chopped nuts

Prepare cake mix according to package directions (except use butter instead of oil). Pour half the batter into a 9x13-inch pan and bake at 350° for 15 minutes. While cake cooks, melt caramel and milk; pour over cooked cake. Top with chocolate chips and nuts. Pour remaining cake batter over top. Bake another 20 to 25 minutes or until top springs back.

Local Favorite

Central REGION

Split Tree Barbecue

Awarded "2014 Best Barbecue"
by Kentucky Pork Producers

115 Wilson Road
Alvaton, KY 42122
270-842-2268

Split Tree BBQ became a reality in 1982 when Jerome Wilson opened his one-man operation selling slow-cooked pork and chicken along with his special secret recipe for beans. Jerome's restaurant gained a huge following and he eventually expanded to include a dining room which is also available for special events. Awarded Best Barbecue in the area many times, Split Tree is an authentic barbecue restaurant offering chicken, pork ribs, sliced pork, and chopped pork sandwiches. Dinners come with barbecue, corn cakes, and your choice of two side orders. Choose from Secret Recipe BBQ Beans, coleslaw, or potato salad.

Sunday: 11:00 am to 8:00 pm
Monday – Thursday: 10:00 am to 8:00 pm
Friday & Saturday: 10:00 am to 9:00 pm

Easy Eggless Potato Salad

5 potatoes, washed well
1 cup chopped celery
½ cup chopped onion
½ cup sweet pickle relish
¼ teaspoon garlic salt
¼ teaspoon celery salt
1 tablespoon prepared mustard
Ground black pepper to taste
¼ cup mayonnaise

Bring a large pot of salted water to a boil. Add potatoes and cook until tender, but still firm, about 15 minutes. Drain, cool, peel and chop. In a large bowl, combine potatoes with celery, onion, relish, garlic salt, celery salt, mustard, pepper and mayonnaise. Mix together well and refrigerate until chilled.

Restaurant Recipe

Kentucky Blackberry Jam Cake

2 cups sugar

1 cup butter, softened

4 eggs

1 teaspoon cinnamon

½ teaspoon cloves

½ teaspoon nutmeg

2 teaspoons baking soda

3 cups flour

2 teaspoons cocoa

1 cup buttermilk

1 cup apple butter

1 cup seedless blackberry jam

Combine sugar, butter and eggs; beat well. Add spices and baking soda and mix. Add flour, cocoa and buttermilk; mix. Add apple butter and jam; mix well. Bake in 3 (8-inch) or 2 (10-inch) pans for 30 minutes at 350°.

Restaurant Recipe

The Augusta General Store

109 Main Street
Augusta, KY 41002
606-756-2525

The Augusta General Store is a unique restaurant and gift shop housed in a building built in the 1700's that survived the Civil War during the battle of Augusta. Located next to the beautiful Ohio River, there are two floors of gifts, antiques, and collectibles. Shop for a special gift while waiting for your food and visit the soda and ice cream bar. Known for their desserts, cakes, pies, cobblers, and cookies, The Augusta General Store also serves sandwiches, hot dinners, and breakfast all day.

7 days a week: 6:00 am to 8:00 pm

Mammy's Kitchen

116 W. Stephen Foster Avenue
Bardstown, KY 40004
502-350-1097
Like us on Facebook!

Mammy's Kitchen is family-owned and family-run, specializing in all-American, country cooking featuring recipes from their family's cookbook, friends, and local favorites. Local favorites include Mammy's Coconut Cream, Chocolate, and Butterscotch Pies made daily. You'll enjoy a wide variety of breakfast, lunch, and dinner menu items, plus daily specials. There's a full bar plus a patio and private dining area. Mammy's Kitchen has been voted "Best Breakfast" (2011 and 2012) and "Best Family" Restaurant (2012) in Nelson County, as well as Third Best Non-Franchise Restaurant in Kentucky by the readers of *Kentucky Living Magazine*.

Monday: 6:30 am to 3:00 pm
Tuesday – Saturday: 6:30 am to 9:00 pm
Sunday: 8:00 am to 2:00 pm
(serving breakfast all day)
Some weekends with entertainment:
9:00 pm to 1:00 am

Coconut Cream Pie

⅔ cup sugar
3 heaping tablespoons cornstarch
½ teaspoon salt
2½ cups milk
3 eggs, separated (reserve whites for Meringue)
1 tablespoon butter
1 teaspoon vanilla
1 cup flaked coconut
1 (8-inch) pie shell, baked

Combine sugar, cornstarch, salt and milk in a saucepan over medium-high heat, whisking until hot. Add egg yolks whisking quickly to prevent them from curdling. Continue to whisk and cook until thickened. Remove from heat. Add butter, vanilla and coconut. Stir well. Pour into baked pie shell.

Meringue:

Reserved 3 egg whites
½ cup sugar
Flaked coconut for topping

Put egg whites in bowl and beat on high until frothy. Add sugar, a little at a time, beating until soft peaks form.

Top pie with meringue. Sprinkle coconut flakes over top. Bake at 350° until peaks turn brown, 5 to 10 minutes.

Restaurant Recipe

Herb Roasted Baby Red Potatoes

2 pounds baby red potatoes
3½ tablespoons olive oil
1 teaspoon kosher salt
½ teaspoon ground black pepper
2½ teaspoons dried oregano
1 teaspoon dried thyme
1 teaspoon dried parsley

Cut potatoes into a large dice, keeping them in cold water to prevent browning; drain, rinse and pat dry. Toss in olive oil until well coated. Spread out on a parchment-lined sheet tray and sprinkle evenly with remaining ingredients. Bake at 350° until cooked through and slightly browned, about 30 to 40 minutes. Makes 5 servings.

Restaurant Recipe

My Old Kentucky Dinner Train

602 North 3rd Street
Bardstown, KY 40004
866-801-3463
www.kydinnertrain.com

Enjoy a bygone era on My Old Kentucky Dinner Train where guests are invited to relax in a spacious, historic depot while awaiting the boarding call. Once on board, guests are seated in a meticulously restored dining car. All tables are set with crisp linens, china, and crystal and offer a picture window to view the scenic Central Kentucky countryside. The award-winning culinary team prepares your gourmet meal on board while an attentive wait staff serves you with a generous side of Southern hospitality.

Sales Office:
Monday – Saturday: 8:30 am to 5:00 pm

Pat's Place Restaurant

125 North 3rd Street
Bardstown, KY 40004
502-348-0010

Family-owned and operated, Pat's Place Restaurant serves fresh food daily at very good prices. The atmosphere is clean and very inviting with a friendly staff to make you feel right at home. Pat's Place features delicious comfort food, made to order just the way you like it. The menu includes salads, chicken, sandwiches, burgers, and veggie burgers. Try the hot plate lunches which are local favorites, and don't miss the homemade pies and cakes. And just for the youngest customers, a kids menu is available.

Monday – Wednesday:
8:00 am to 3:00 pm
Thursday – Saturday: 8:00 am to 1:00 pm
Sunday (breakfast only):
8:00 am to 1:00 pm

Homemade Meatloaf

5 pounds ground beef
1 large red onion, diced
1 large green bell pepper, diced
½ cup sweet pickle relish
½ cup pepper relish
3 eggs, beaten
Salt and pepper to taste
2 cups crushed crackers and/or breadcrumbs
1 cup tomato juice

Mix all ingredients together, except tomato juice. Form into a loaf. Pour tomato juice over loaf. Bake at 350° for 2 hours.

Restaurant Recipe

Bourbon Brussels Sprouts

2 tablespoons butter

4 slices bacon, chopped ½-inch pieces

**1 large green apple, large dice
(do not remove peel)**

¼ cup dried cranberries

¼ cup brown sugar

¼ cup bourbon

1¼ pounds Brussels sprouts, halved

Heat butter in saucepan. Render bacon in hot butter for about 2 minutes. Reduce heat to medium-low and continue to cook until browned. Add remaining ingredients in order, stirring well after each. Cook until Brussels sprouts are brown, about 8 to 10 minutes.

Restaurant Recipe

The Rickhouse Restaurant & Lounge

**112 Xavier Drive
Bardstown, KY 40004
502-348-2832
www.therickhouse-bardstown.com**

At The Rickhouse, it's all about the flavor. Their recipes are one of a kind, showcasing the town's bourbon heritage. The dishes contain only quality ingredients, marinated in The Rickhouse's showcase bourbon glazes. In the dishes not prepared with that unique bourbon glaze, you will find creamy, rich sauces and mouth-watering seasonings. Local favorites are the twelve-cheese macaroni and the seasoned potatoes. In addition to outstanding food, The Rickhouse offers a complete collection of the best bourbons along with a changing selection of wines and brews inspired by seasonal flavors. Make the trip to Bardstown and visit The Rickhouse Restaurant & Lounge; you won't be disappointed.

Tuesday – Saturday: 4:00 pm to 10:00 pm

Bee Spring Restaurant

7879 Kentucky Highway 259 North
Bee Spring, KY 42207
270-286-0222

Located in one of the area's most pleasant settings, Bee Spring Restaurant (aka BSR or just plain—the rest'urnt) is known for its delightful staff and down-home, back road, country cooking. This unique restaurant features a wide array of great food selections, made from only the freshest and highest quality ingredients, with something sure to please every member of your group. For nearly sixty years, Bee Spring Restaurant has established itself as one of the area's favorite culinary destinations and is sure to offer you a pleasant and unique dining experience every time you visit. Please stop in soon.

Sunday – Thursday: 6:00 am to 9:00 pm
Friday & Saturday: 6:00 am to 10:00 pm

Bee Spring Delight

1 flour tortilla per serving
Oil for frying
Powdered sugar
Sugar
Cinnamon
2 scoops (or a swirl) vanilla ice cream
Chocolate syrup

Cut tortilla into sixths or eighths. Deep fry to lightly brown. Remove to drain. Sprinkle with a mixture of powdered sugar, sugar and cinnamon to your taste. Place ice cream in a serving bowl. Position triangles around ice cream. Drizzle with chocolate syrup. Enjoy!

Restaurant Recipe

Bee Spring Baked Potato

1 baking potato, baked
Swiss or American cheese
Freshly grilled chicken breast, sliced or diced
Grilled onions
Bacon
Butter
Sour cream

Split potato and open wide. Top with the following ingredients in order, cheese, chicken, onions, bacon, butter and sour cream. Enjoy!

Restaurant Recipe

Mediterranean Tilapia

Vegetable Medley:

3 large tomatoes, thinly sliced

1 (14-ounce) can artichoke hearts, leaves separated by hand

2 teaspoons capers

1 teaspoon chopped garlic

Salt and pepper to taste

2 teaspoons grated Parmesan

4 large basil leaves, thinly sliced

2 ounces (4 tablespoons) olive oil

In a large bowl, combine all Vegetable Medley ingredients and let set for 2 hours.

Tilapia:

4 tilapia fillets

Salt and pepper

½ cup white wine

1 tablespoon cold butter

Chopped parsley for garnish

1 lemon, cut into 4 wedges for garnish

Spray a large oven-safe skillet with oil. Add fillets, season with salt and pepper to taste, and add Vegetable Medley on top. Add wine and bake at 500° for 25 minutes, or until tilapia is firm. Remove tilapia to a plate. Add butter to remaining mixture in skillet; stir till butter melts. Top tilapia with mixture; garnish with chopped parsley and lemon wedge. Bon Appétit!

Restaurant Recipe

The Bistro

1129 College Street
Bowling Green, KY 42101
270-781-9646
thebistrobg.com

Located just two blocks from serene Fountain Square, The Bistro welcomes you to one-of-the-kind dining. The two-story restored 1893 Fletcher House plays host to both first-rate meals and service whether you are enjoying dinner for two in the restaurant or drinks with friends in the bar. Classically European, Comfortably American!

LUNCH:
Monday – Friday: 11:00 am to 4:00 pm
DINNER:
Monday – Thursday: 5:00 pm to 9:00 pm
Friday & Saturday: 5:00 pm to 10:00 pm
BRUNCH:
Sunday: 10:30 am to 3:00 pm

CambridgeMarketandCafe.com

Cambridge
MARKET & CAFÉ

@CambridgeBGKY

Cambridge Market and Café

Cambridge Square Shopping Center
830 Fairview Avenue
Bowling Green, KY 42101
270-782-9366 • 270-782-9367
cambridgemarketandcafe.com
Follow us on Facebook and Twitter

One of Bowling Green's most iconic cafés is where the locals eat. Cambridge Market is Southern comfort meets contemporary cuisine. A family-owned restaurant that features local ingredients and regional flair, Cambridge Market has it all: made-from-scratch soups, sandwiches, casseroles, entrées, pies, cakes, and cheesecake; quick, casual dining for both lunch and dinner; gourmet catering at a fraction of the cost; and a healthy dose of Southern hospitality. For business lunches, family outings, and everything in between, Cambridge Market is the place for local flavor.

Monday – Friday: 9:00 am to 7:00 pm
Saturday: 9:00 am to 2:00 pm

Cambridge Banana Pudding

Usually made by Ruth

3 cups milk

¼ cup all-purpose flour

½ cup sugar

3 eggs, separated (reserve egg whites)

1 teaspoon vanilla extract

1 (16-ounce) box vanilla wafers

4 to 6 ripe bananas, peeled and sliced

In a medium saucepan over low heat, add milk. Slowly add flour, whisking continually to avoid lumps. Slowly stir in sugar, whisking continually until fully dissolved. Use a fork and break up the egg yolks. Slowly add egg yolks to saucepan, whisking continually to avoid making scrambled eggs. It's very important to stay with the cooking process at this point. Keep stirring.

Increase heat gradually to medium as you constantly whisk the pudding mixture. Continue to stir constantly as it thickens. Using a candy thermometer, bring the mixture up to 170°; remove from heat, but continue to stir. Add vanilla, stirring occasionally as it cools down. Cool completely before assembling the banana pudding.

Preheat oven to 350°. When pudding is cool, spread a light layer in a deep 4-quart casserole dish. Add a layer of vanilla wafers. Add a layer of sliced bananas. Add a layer of pudding mixture, spreading it out to the edges of the dish. Repeat the layers, using all ingredients (reserve 5 to 6 vanilla wafers for top), ending with a layer of the pudding mixture on top. Crumble reserved wafers and sprinkle on top.

Meringue:

Reserved egg whites, room temperature

⅛ teaspoon cream of tartar

¼ cup sugar

Place room temperature egg whites in a glass or metal mixing bowl. Using an electric mixer, beat egg whites until frothy. Add cream of tartar. Increase mixer speed and beat until egg whites form soft peaks. Add sugar. Continue to whip, increasing speed as needed, until egg whites thicken and form firm peaks. Do not over work as it will cause the meringue to lose volume. Use a spatula and gently spread meringue over pudding mixture. Gently dab spatula up and down in the meringue to form small swirls and peaks.

Place dish in the preheated oven and bake 10 to 15 minutes. Watch carefully so meringue doesn't burn; it just needs to be slightly toasted and browned. Remove from oven, let cool, then refrigerate until cold. Serve. (A lot of times we use whipped topping in place of meringue. Make it your way depending on your preference.)

Restaurant Recipe

Lisa's Fifth Street Diner

430 Center Street
Bowling Green, KY 42101
270-904-1467

Welcome to Lisa's Fifth Street Diner where eating is just like sitting at mama's table. Owner Lisa Parker, also known as the "Radio Lady," serves the finest fresh produce, country ham, and pork from local growers and farmers. Sit down at the table and enjoy meatloaf, fried chicken, catfish, or salmon patties. Don't forget the desserts which are always made fresh daily. Listen for Lisa on the radio each morning letting everyone know what is being served that day. Then drop in for an outstanding meal.

Monday – Thursday: 5:00 am to 2:00 pm
Friday: 5:00 am to 8:00 pm
Saturday: 5:30 am to 2:00 pm
Sunday: 6:00 am to 2:00 pm

Broccoli Salad

3 cups fresh broccoli
½ cup shredded American cheese
½ cup shredded Monterey Jack cheese
½ cup diced red onions
½ cup diced tomatoes
2 cups mayonnaise
2 tablespoons distilled white vinegar
¼ cup white sugar
1 teaspoon salt
¼ teaspoon black pepper

Combine all ingredients; mix well. Refrigerate 30 minutes before serving. Add additional mayonnaise if salad is too dry.

Restaurant Recipe

THINKSTOCK/ISTOCK/ UTAH778

Riley's Bakery

819 US 31-W By Pass
Bowling Green, KY 42101
270-842-7636
www.rileysbakerybg.com
Find us on Facebook

Walk through the doors and smell the wonders of a good, old-fashioned bakery. That is what happens every time you step into Riley's, a family-owned business that has been in Bowling Green for seventy plus years. They make their products from scratch using only the highest quality ingredients. Riley's offers a full line of bakery products—everything from donuts and breakfast items to cookies, brownies, and cupcakes; breads, pies, and cobblers; birthday, graduation and wedding cakes—all made fresh in house. Eat delicious sandwiches made like your grandmother used to make, because they were developed from their own mother's recipes.

The tea cookies are a favorite of all generations. Try the Hungarian coffee cake, a delight not only for yourself, but also makes the perfect gift. The brownies and blondies are pure heaven. Riley's Bakery is a destination not only for visitors, but is also a favorite of locals. Many people make Riley's one of their first stops when returning home to relive the memories of growing up or living in Bowling Green.

Monday – Friday: 6:45 am to 5:30 pm
Saturday: 6:45 am to 2:30 pm

THINKSTOCK/ISTOCK/CHARLES BRUTLAG

Cream Cheese Cupcakes

2 (8-ounce) packages cream cheese, softened

¾ cup sugar

2 eggs

1 teaspoon vanilla

1 (12-ounce) box vanilla wafers

1 (20-ounce) can blueberry pie filling

Combine cream cheese and sugar until creamy. Add eggs and vanilla; mix well. Fill a full-size muffin tin with cupcake liners. Place 1 vanilla wafer in each liner. Spoon 2 tablespoons cream cheese mixture over vanilla wafer. Bake at 350° for about 20 minutes or until set. Cool completely. Spoon 1 tablespoon pie filling on top. Makes about 24 cupcakes.

Local Favorite

Sour Cream Fruit Dip

1 cup sour cream

½ teaspoon cinnamon

½ teaspoon nutmeg

Dash cloves

1 teaspoon vanilla

½ teaspoon rum extract

2 tablespoons sugar

Combine all ingredients; mix well. Chill at least 1 hour or overnight. (Will keep for up to 1 month in the refrigerator).

Local Favorite

Oatmeal Cookies

1 cup seedless raisins

1 cup water

¾ cup shortening

1½ cups sugar

2 eggs

1 teaspoon vanilla

2½ cups flour

½ teaspoon baking powder

1 teaspoon baking soda

1 teaspoon salt

1 teaspoon cinnamon

½ teaspoon cloves

2 cups rolled oats

½ cup chopped nuts

Simmer raisins and water in a small saucepan over low heat 20 minutes (raisins should be plump). Drain liquid into a measuring cup; add water, if needed, to make ½ cup.

Preheat oven to 400°. Cream shortening, sugar, eggs and vanilla. Stir in raisin liquid. In a separate bowl, combine flour, baking powder, baking soda, salt and spices. Add to creamed mixture. Stir in oats, nuts and raisins. Drop by rounded teaspoonfuls about 2 inches apart on a lightly treated baking sheet. Bake 8 to 10 minutes.

Local Favorite

THINKSTOCK/ ISTOCK/JOEL ALBRIZIO

Smokey Pig Bar-B-Q

2520 Louisville Road
Bowling Green, KY 42101
www.smokeypigbbq.com
270-781-1712

Located on Smokey Pig Road, a side street that runs parallel to Louisville Road, you will find Smokey Pig Bar-B-Q sitting atop a one hundred-foot-high river bluff on the Barren River. To find them, get off I-65 at exit 28 then get in the left lane which will take you to Louisville Road (Highway 31 West). Again, get into the left lane and you will see Smokey Pig in approximately 1 mile on the left. Family-owned and operated since 1969, their delicious pork and chicken is cooked over hickory coals and basted with Smokey's homemade vinegar-based sauce. You will also enjoy their homemade mild sauce and rib sauce. For a delicious meal and great scenery—the rear dining room overlooks the river—don't miss Smokey Pig Bar-B-Q where the Huffer family and their team will make you feel right at home.

Tuesday – Saturday: 10:30 am to 7:00 pm

Sausage Cheese Dip

1 pound ground sausage, hot or mild

1 pound Velveeta cheese

1 pound Velveeta Mexican cheese, hot or mild

1 to 2 large crowns broccoli

1 (14.5-ounce) can crushed or diced tomatoes

Brown sausage; drain. While sausage is browning, cube both kinds of cheese and place in slow cooker set to low. While cheese melts, steam broccoli until tender. Add sausage and broccoli to slow cooker with tomatoes. Cook until cheese is completely melted, stirring occasionally. Serve with tortilla chips for dipping or pour over chips and serve.

Family Favorite

7 Layer Salad

1 head lettuce, shredded

½ head cauliflower, pieces

½ bunch broccoli, pieces

½ green bell pepper, chopped

1 (15-ounce) can green peas (English peas), drained

4 boiled eggs, sliced, optional

½ cup shredded cheese

Bacon bits to taste

Layer ingredients in a clear serving bowl in order presented.

Dressing:

1 cup mayonnaise

1 cup ranch salad dressing

Combine dressing ingredients and pour over 7 Layer Salad. Serve immediately.

Restaurant Recipe

Sweet Temptations Bakery, Café and Catering

Fairview Plaza
600 US 31 West Bypass, Suite 3A
Bowling Green, KY 42101
270-904-4210
www.sweettemptationsbgky.com

Sweet Temptations Bakery is the place to go when you want to satisfy your sweet tooth or are hungry for brunch or lunch. You are guaranteed to love their breakfast pastries, coffees, espressos, smoothies, homemade chicken salad, pimento cheese, wraps, grilled sandwiches, soups, salads, homemade sourdough bread, and daily lunch specials. In addition to great meals, Sweet Temptations can take care of all your catering, cake, floral, decorating, linen, and coordinating needs. They offer gift baskets, homemade candies and cookies, cheesecakes, pies, sweet breads, and much (much!) more. They will cater any occasion at any location, offer custom special-order cakes for all occasions, plus cakes and pies whole or by the slice. Be sure to stop by and let owner Dafnel DeVasier and her crew make your day a little sweeter.

Monday – Friday: 7:30 am to 5:30 pm
Saturday: 8:00 am to 3:00 pm

Betty's OK Country Cooking

**2339 Campbellsville Road
Columbia, KY 42728
270-384-5664
Hot Bar Menu:
www.columbiamagazine.com**

Walk into Betty's OK Country Cooking and you will hear more than one voice say, "Hello!", "How ya'll doing?" or "Just have a seat where ever you like, we will be right with you." You will feel right at home from the moment you walk through the door. The hot bar offers entrées daily with a variety of home-style vegetables. There is also a full menu available featuring lots of desserts made daily. Don't miss Betty's Famous "Sand" Pie. If you've never eaten at Betty's drop by and give them a try. They may not know you the first time, but when you go back, they'll probably call you by name (or at least remember what you drink).

Monday – Saturday: 5:00 am to 9:00 pm

Betty's Famous "Sand" Pie

Crust:

**1 cup flour
1 stick margarine, melted
¼ cup pecan pieces**

Combine crust ingredients; spread into a 9-inch pie pan; bake at 350° to light golden brown. Cool.

First Layer:

**1 (8-ounce) package cream cheese, softened
1 cup powdered sugar
¼ cup whipped topping**

Mix till creamy; spread in cooled crust.

Second Layer:

**1 (3-ounce) box vanilla pudding
¼ cup pecan pieces
1½ cups milk**

Mix till thick; spread over First Layer.

Third Layer:

Top with whipped cream and pecan pieces.

Restaurant Recipe

Sweet Potato Casserole

2 (29-ounce) cans or 4 (15-ounce) cans
sweet potatoes

3 eggs, beaten

1½ cups sugar

1 stick butter, melted

1 tablespoon vanilla

Drain sweet potatoes well and mash. Mix sweet potatoes and all other ingredients together and spread into 12x17-inch coated baking dish. Bake covered at 350° for 20 to 25 minutes. Remove and stir.

Topping:

1 stick butter, melted

2 cups brown sugar

1½ cups flour

½ cup chopped pecans

Mix well. Spread topping over sweet potatoes. Return to oven to bake until golden brown, about 10 minutes.

Restaurant Recipe

Back Home Restaurant

251 West Dixie Avenue
Elizabethtown, KY 42701
270-769-2800
www.backhomerestaurant.com

Owned and operated by the Fulkerson family for the past thirty years, Back Home Restaurant is a place unlike any other. They are located in an 1872 Italian-style home offering a unique dining and retail experience. Nestled among civil war nostalgia and historical Southern charm, the quaint atmosphere and Southern-infused menu are sure to please everyone. They also offer full service catering and a newly added boutique. Always remember, you can go "Back Home" again!

Sunday & Monday: 11:00 am to 3:00 pm
Tuesday – Saturday: 11:00 am to 9:00 pm

Cobbler's Café

**125 East Dixie Avenue
Elizabethtown, KY 42701
270-982-2233 (CAFE)**

Cobbler's Café is a small coffee shop and café in historic downtown Elizabethtown serving a full breakfast and lunch every day except Sunday. Cobbler's Café serves a variety of soups, salads, sandwiches, wraps, scones, desserts, and cobblers. The namesake dessert is made from a family recipe several generations old. Jayme and Kristi Burden have been serving up some of the best coffee, desserts, and foods since they opened the café in the fall of 2004. The building was a shoe repair shop for over fifty years, prior to that it was home to several different businesses, including a doctor's office. The building was built in 1878 for two local doctors. Today, Cobbler's Café serves blueberry, blackberry, peach, strawberry or other seasonal cobblers made from scratch and served with ice cream. Sit back, relax, and enjoy some conversation as the food is freshly prepared for you.

Monday – Saturday: 7:30 am to 3:30 pm

Vinegar Slaw

**1 head cabbage, grated
1 onion, grated
1 green bell pepper, finely chopped
½ cup salad oil
¼ cup sugar
½ cup vinegar
1 teaspoon salt**

Mix all ingredients. Chill and serve.

Restaurant Recipe

Lemon Tea Bread

½ cup shortening, softened

1 cup sugar

2 eggs

1½ cups flour

1½ teaspoons baking powder

¼ teaspoon salt

½ cup milk

Grated rind of 1 lemon

Cream shortening with an electric mixer at medium speed; gradually add sugar, beating well. While continuing to beat, add eggs, 1 at a time. Combine dry ingredients and gradually add to creamed mixture, alternating with milk. Stir in lemon rind. Bake in a 5x9-inch loaf pan at 350° for 50 to 55 minutes. Cool before glazing.

Glaze:

Juice of 1 lemon

1¼ cups powdered sugar

Stir together and pour over cooled bread. Slice and serve.

Restaurant Recipe

Cobbler's Best Chili

2 pounds ground beef, browned and drained

½ cup finely chopped onion

1 teaspoon salt

1 teaspoon pepper

2 cups chopped tomatoes

1 (9-ounce) can tomato sauce

1 (10-ounce) can cream of mushroom soup

3 tablespoons mild chili powder

2 cups hot kidney beans

2 cups water

¾ cup broken dry spaghetti

In a large pot over medium heat, combine cooked beef, onion, salt and pepper. Mix well. Add tomatoes, tomato sauce, soup, chili powder, beans and water. Stir to mix then heat to almost boiling over medium heat. Add dry spaghetti and cook just until spaghetti is soft.

Restaurant Recipe

Family Buffet

121 Towne Drive
Elizabethtown, KY 42701
270-763-0091
www.familybuffetelizabethtown.com

When you are looking for the best in authentic Chinese cuisine, come visit the Chinese buffet at Family Buffet, a family-owned restaurant operating in Elizabethtown for more than fifteen years. They offer customers a wide variety of authentic Chinese cuisine including Mongolian BBQ grill, sushi, seafood and the area's largest selection of traditional Chinese fare. The family atmosphere will have you feeling right at home. Family Buffet is staffed with friendly caring employees making it the perfect place for small or large groups or families with children. The warm, friendly dining room provides a comfortable place to enjoy the area's finest Chinese delicacies with family and friends.

Monday – Thursday:
11:00 am to 10:00 pm
Friday & Saturday: 11:00 am to 11:00 pm
Sunday: 1:00 pm to 9:00 pm

Sautéed Green Beans

1 pound fresh green beans
Oil for deep frying
⅓ teaspoon sesame oil
½ teaspoon chopped garlic
½ teaspoon chicken base
1½ tablespoons cooking wine
½ teaspoon thick soy sauce
⅓ teaspoon sugar
⅓ teaspoon salt

Rinse beans well and snap ends, leaving beans whole. Prepare a large stockpot of boiling water. Heat oil for frying to 350°. Drop green beans in oil for 30 seconds then boiling water to remove oil. Heat a large pan. Add sesame oil, garlic and green beans; stir fry to desired tenderness. Add remaining ingredients. Heat through and serve.

Restaurant Recipe

CIVIL WAR
CANNON BALL
BELOW UPPER WINDOW
FIRED FROM CEMETERY
BY MORGAN'S MEN

RE-PLACED CIVIL WAR CANNONBALL

Elizabethtown

Fired from a cannon in 1862, this cannonball became lodged in a building more than twenty-five years later. Why such a long journey? Confederate soldiers attacked Elizabethtown, raining more than one hundred cannonballs on the town. One lodged in the outside wall of the Depp Building on the town square. When the building burned down in 1887, a visionary resident, Miss Annie Nourse, offered twenty-five cents to the local boy who could find the cannonball. The cannonball was successfully recovered from the rubble and safeguarded by Miss Nourse. Years after the building was rebuilt, the cannonball was placed back into the second story of the wall as close as they could approximate to the original location.

Elizabethtown, known as E-Town, is full of history and character. In addition to the cannonball, there are many interesting things to see—the Hardin County History Museum, Lincoln Heritage House, Swope's Cars of Yesteryear Museum, and much more.

www.touretown.com • 800-437-0092

Kingdom Buffet

611 West Popular Street Suite A-15
Elizabethtown, KY 42701
270-982-3898

A Chinese family restaurant, Kingdom Buffet was established in 2006. With the goal of serving the community in a comfortable, clean environment with friendly service, they feature Chinese cuisine made fresh every day. On weekends, enjoy the seafood and hibachi grill. Kingdom Buffet accepts all major credit cards and offers military discount. Call for all your catering needs.

Monday – Thursday:
11:00 am to 10:00 pm
Friday & Saturday: 11:00 am to 11:00 pm
Sunday: 11:00 am to 9:00 pm

Crab Rangoon

1 small onion
¼ cup chopped celery
¼ teaspoon minced green onion
1 small carrot
¼ (8-ounce) can water chestnuts
Sugar to taste
3 (8-ounce) packages cream cheese, softened
¼ pound crabmeat
144 wonton wrappers
1 egg, beaten
Vegetable oil for frying

Grind together (using blender or food processor) onion, celery, green onion, carrot, water chestnuts and sugar. Combine with cream cheese and crabmeat. Squeeze out as much water as possible and refrigerate overnight. Place a teaspoonful of mixture in the middle of each wonton, fold into a triangle, and seal edges with beaten egg. Deep fry in vegetable oil until golden brown. Serves 24.

Restaurant Recipe

Classic Meatballs

1 pound ground beef

1 pound ground pork

1 pound ground veal

½ cup freshly grated Pecorino Romano cheese

½ cup freshly grated Parmesan cheese

4 large eggs, beaten

¼ cup chopped roasted garlic

1 cup heavy cream (40% fat)

1 cup Italian-style panko

½ cup Italian-style breadcrumbs

In a large mixing bowl, combine all ingredients and mix well. Shape into meatballs the size of golf balls (makes approximately 48). Cover and refrigerate for at least 1 hour. Cook meatballs directly in your favorite sauce.

(Chef's Hint: If you're not going to cook all the meatballs at once, place the remainder on a parchment-lined cookie sheet and place in freezer for 30 minutes or until frozen. Then place in a zip-top storage container and keep frozen. Add them to your next dish directly from the freezer.)

Restaurant Recipe

Michael's Italian Restaurant

1704 North Dixie Highway
Elizabethtown, KY 42701
In Towne Mall
270-506-0333
www.michaelsitalianrestaurantky.com

Michael's Italian Restaurant brings traditional Italian cuisine to Central Kentucky. Michael's Italian is owned and managed by Chef Michael Messina and his partner Mark Bennett, along with their families. Chef Michael is proud to present his great-grandmother's cooking secrets to all patrons, her photos are even on the wall. The food is made from scratch with many ingredients imported from Italy. The families pride themselves on being one of the few locally-owned restaurants in the Hardin County area. This outstanding restaurant features traditional Italian cuisine in a menu offering appetizers, salads, pizzas, pastas, entrées and homemade desserts.

Sunday: 10:30 am to 5:30 pm
Monday – Friday: 11:00 am to 9:00 pm
Saturday: 8:00 am to 9:00 pm

Yesterday's Café & Tea Room

264 Main Street
Florence, KY 41042
859-594-4TEA (4832)
www.yesterdayscafeandtearoom.com

Located in a 120-year-old historic building in Olde Florence, Yesterday's provides the perfect escape for customers wanting a peaceful gathering place that has that old time

charm and feel. Whether you enjoy the elegantly decorated tea room for brunch, lunch, or afternoon tea, or just pop by for a delicious pastry in the casual café, their attentive staff is there to please. A visit to the café or tea room wouldn't be complete without time to browse the well-stocked gift boutique. There you'll find the tri-state's largest selection of tea and tea-related wares, plus some more wonderful surprises. When the weather is fair, enjoy Yesterday's beautiful courtyard.

Tuesday – Friday:
8:00 am to 5:00 pm
Saturday & Sunday:
10:00 am to 4:00 pm

Matcha (Green Tea) Macaroons

Cookies:

1 cup powdered sugar

½ cup plus 1 tablespoon almond flour

2¼ teaspoons Ancient Leaf Matcha

2 egg whites, at room temperature

5 tablespoons sugar

Line 2 cookie sheets with parchment paper. Combine powdered sugar, almond flour and matcha powder in food processor. Pulse into a fine powder, scraping bowl occasionally. Sift mixture into medium bowl. Beat egg whites in large bowl with electric mixture at medium speed until foamy. Gradually add sugar, beating at high speed 3 minutes until mixture forms stiff, shiny peaks. Add half of flour mixture to egg whites; stir with spatula to combine (about 12 to 15 strokes). Attach ½-inch plain tip to piping bag. Scoop batter into bag. Pipe 1-inch circles about 2 inches apart onto prepared cookie sheets. Rap cookie sheet on flat surface to release air bubbles. Rest, uncovered, until tops harden slightly (20 to 30 minutes). Preheat oven to 350°. Place in center rack of oven. Bake 15 to 18 minutes, rotating halfway through baking time. Cool completely on cookie sheets.

Filling:

4 ounces semisweet chocolate chips

¼ cup whipping cream

1 tablespoon butter

Place chocolate chips in medium bowl. Heat cream and butter in a small saucepan; pour over chocolate. Let stand 3 minutes. Stir until smooth. Let stand 15 minutes. Match same size cookies; pipe or spread filling on flat side of one cookie and top with other. Makes 15 to 18 macaroons.

Restaurant Recipe

The Whistle Stop Restaurant

216 East Main Street • Glendale, KY 42740
270-369-8586
www.whistlestopky.com

The Whistle Stop is a family-owned restaurant and gift shop established in 1975. Serving true, made-from-scratch dishes and desserts, Whistle Stop has been featured in *Southern Living* magazine, and voted Favorite Non-Franchise Restaurant in Kentucky the past five years. The restaurant is in a one hundred-year-old building sitting beside the railroad track with an original log cabin attached. The log cabin holds the General Store and a place to sit while you wait. There is plenty to do when you come to historic Glendale to eat and visit the antique and gift shops.

Tuesday – Saturday: 11:00 am to 9:00 pm

Shepherd's Pie

Served in the winter months as a weekly special.

2½ pounds ground beef

Salt and pepper

1 (2-pound) bag frozen mixed vegetables

½ pound (2 sticks) margarine

2 teaspoons minced garlic

8 tablespoons flour

4 to 5 cups hot beef broth (made with hot water and beef base)

2 tablespoons Worcestershire sauce

1 large batch (4 to 6 cups) mashed potatoes with sour cream added

Season meat with salt and pepper; cook in a skillet, chopping well, until cooked through. Drain. Lightly steam vegetables. Melt margarine in a skillet over medium-high heat; whisk in garlic and flour; cook, stirring constantly, 2 minutes. Whisk in 4 cups broth. Add Worcestershire sauce, and cook until thick. (It should not be real thick, add more broth if it is too thick.) Stir in vegetables and meat. Taste and season if needed. Spread in a large sheet pan and heat in oven at 350° till hot and bubbly, about 30 to 45 minutes. Top with hot mashed potatoes and return to oven until lightly brown, about 5 to 10 minutes. Makes about 12 servings.

Restaurant Recipe

Pecan Pie

Called Kentucky Pie, this is served daily with the chocolate chips added.

1 cup brown sugar

1½ cups sugar

1 tablespoon flour

½ cup melted butter

2 eggs

2 tablespoons milk

1 teaspoon vanilla

½ cup chocolate chips, optional

1 (9-inch) pie shell, unbaked

1½ cups chopped pecans

Mix both sugars and flour. Add melted butter. Add eggs, milk and vanilla; mix well. Add chocolate chips, if desired. Pour into unbaked pie shell. Sprinkle chopped pecans evenly over top. Bake at 350° about 45 minutes.

For 3 Pie Crusts:

3 cups plain flour

1 teaspoon salt

1 cup lard

½ cup warm water

½ tablespoon vinegar

Stir flour and salt together; blend in lard. Make a well in the middle, pour in liquids. Mix by hand until blended, roll out.

Restaurant Recipes

Down Home Cookin'

112 North Main Street
Greensburg, KY 42743
270-405-3101

Down Home Cookin' is a small catering business started more than ten years ago by Bobby Marcum after many years cooking and catering with his grandmother, Geneva Penick. Bobby stood by her side for many years watching her cook from scratch and wondering if he could ever cook like that one day. Now he, and everyone around, knows that Bobby can indeed cook as well as his grandmother because he is keeping her dream alive. Primarily a catering company, Down Home Cookin' serves lunch two days a week and offers an all-you-can-eat buffet Friday nights. Make plans to be there one of those days because the effort is worth it.

Wednesday & Thursday:
10:00 am to 2:00 pm
Friday: 4:00 pm to 8:00 pm

Butterscotch Pie

⅔ cup brown sugar
⅓ cup white sugar
2 tablespoons cornstarch
Pinch salt
3 eggs, separated
(reserve whites for Meringue)
1½ cups milk
½ stick (¼ cup) butter, softened
1 teaspoon vanilla
1 (9-inch) pie shell, baked

Mix dry ingredients together in a small bowl. In a large microwave-safe mixing bowl, beat egg yolks; add milk. Stir in dry ingredients. Add butter and vanilla. Microwave on high 8 minutes, stirring every 2 minutes to prevent lumps. Pour into pie shell. Top with prepared meringue, sealing edges. Bake at 350° until brown, 5 to 10 minutes.

Meringue:

½ cup cold water
½ cup sugar
1 tablespoon cornstarch
Reserved eggs whites from 3 eggs
1 teaspoon vanilla

In a saucepan, cook water, sugar and cornstarch until it makes a paste; cool. Beat egg whites until still peaks form. Add paste mixture and vanilla; beat well.

Restaurant Recipe

DERBY CLOCK
Louisville

The forty-foot-tall Louisville Clock was designed by sculptor Barney Bright to look like a giant wind-up toy. Ornamental columns support an elevated eight-lane race track and a grandstand of cheering fans. Each day at noon and 6:00 pm, a bugle announces the beginning of a race between five hand-carved statues of George Rogers Clark, Daniel Boone, Thomas Jefferson, King Louis XVI of France, and the Belle of Louisville.

The clock has been an iconic Louisville landmark since 1976 but has been plagued with many problems over the years. Its location was changed several times, then it was dismantled and placed in storage in the early 1990's due to mechanical issues and lack of funding.

After rusting away for almost twenty years, the whimsical, beautiful, folk art clock received a $1 million restoration and is back to its original splendor. In 2012, the clock finally found a permanent home at Theater Square. Stop by and watch the next race—it is truly a sight to behold.

Theater Square • 4th Street • Louisville, KY 40202

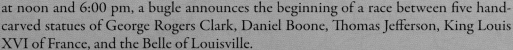

Longhunters Coffee and Tea Company

115-117 South Public Square
Greensburg, KY 42743
270-932-2351
www.longhunterscoffeeandtea.com

Located in a renovated hardware store on the town square, Longhunters Coffee and Tea Company offers handcrafted eats and specialty drinks with menu items named for historical figures and places in the area. Longhunters' selection of hot herbal teas and hand-crafted mocha and latté specialty drinks is addictive. Owners Colonel Bill Landrum and his wife, Justine, offer a selection of hand-crafted hearty sandwiches, full-plated fresh salads, hand-made crêpes, pinto beans, pulled pork, and many other "On the Square" specials. Two local favorites are the Longhunters Hot Brown (turkey breast served atop a cornmeal hoecake smothered in a cheesy Mornay sauce) and the General Nathaniel Greene (turkey breast, provolone, and roasted red peppers on sun-dried tomato bread dressed with herbed oil). A large selection of desserts is always on display . . . and they now offer custom catering and a full Sunday buffet.

Monday – Thursday: 8:00 am to 2:00 pm
Friday & Saturday: 8:00 am to 7:00 pm
Sunday Brunch: 10:30 am to 1:00 pm

Longhunters Hot Brown

Open–Faced Sandwich:

18 to 20 strips bacon

8 to 9 tomato slices

Sun-dried tomato breadcrumbs mixed with fresh chopped parsley flakes

Preheat oven to 300°. Cook bacon in oven 10 minutes or until cooked; drain on paper towels. When bacon is cool, cut in half to make 36 to 40 pieces. Set oven 350°. Prepare Turkey, Sauce and Cornmeal Hoecake as directed below.

For each hot brown, cover hoecake with turkey and ladle sauce over the top. Place 5 pieces of bacon in middle of sauce forming a star. Top with a tomato slice and breadcrumbs mixed with parsley flakes. Place in oven and cook until bubbles form around edge. Serves 8 to 9.

Turkey:

1 (5- to 6-pound) boneless turkey breast roast (Perdue)

½ stick unsalted butter, softened

Kosher salt and freshly ground pepper

Rub turkey breast with butter and season with salt and pepper. Place in a 6-inch-deep roasting pan. Cover with foil and roast 1½ to 1¾ hours at 350°, until a thermometer inserted into the center of the breast reaches 160°. Remove from oven and cool 20 to 25 minutes before slicing into ½-inch slices.

Sauce:

1 (49-ounce) can of béchamel cream sauce (Campbell's)

½ tablespoon garlic powder

½ tablespoon onion powder

½ tablespoon mustard

¼ teaspoon freshly ground pepper

8 ounces shredded sharp white Cheddar (Brickman's)

2 ounces (or 3 slices) grated pepper jack cheese

Place béchamel in a large saucepan. Whisk in seasonings and both cheeses. Place food pan on warmer (or saucepan on stove over medium-low heat) until cheese has melted.

Cornmeal Hoecake:

1 cup all-purpose cornmeal

1 cup self-rising flour

¼ teaspoon salt

1 teaspoon baking powder

½ cup buttermilk

¼ cup water

3 eggs

6 tablespoons unsalted butter, softened

¼ cup canola oil

In a bowl, combine cornmeal, flour, salt and baking powder. Whisk in buttermilk, water, eggs and butter. Heat oil in a cast-iron skillet over medium heat. Cook hoecakes, 1 at a time, each about 4- to 5-inches round. Makes 8 to 9 cakes.

Restaurant Recipe

Make It Snappy

Snappy Tomato Pizza

106 West Court Street
Greensburg, KY 42743
270-932-2020
www.snappytomatopizza.com

Snappy Tomato Pizza is Greensburg's neighborhood pizzeria and is locally owned and operated by Peggy and John Frank and Karen and Bill Gilpin. As longtime friends and coworkers, they would often brainstorm ideas for their town. After long hours and hard work, they opened Snappy Tomato Pizza in March 2009. You will love the all-u-can-eat buffet featuring pizza, pasta, salad, and more. Or, get your pizza by SNAPPY delivery—call or order online at Snappytomatopizza.com. What is the SNAPPY difference? Pizza dough that is made fresh daily, fresh (never frozen) mozzarella cheese, special SNAPPY pizza sauce made from fresh-packed tomatoes, SNAPPY select meats, and the finest selection of fresh vegetables. When you visit historic Greensburg, get snappy with a Snappy Tomato Pizza.

Weekdays: 9:00 am to 9:00 pm
Weekends: 9:00 am to 10:00 pm

SKI-Glazed Apple Dumplings

2 (8-ounce) cans crescent rolls
2 Granny Smith apples, peeled, cored and cut into 8 wedges
2 sticks butter
1½ cups sugar
1 teaspoon vanilla
1 teaspoon ground cinnamon
1 can SKI or Mountain Dew
Vanilla ice cream, optional (but you'll wish you did)

Preheat oven to 350°. Unfold and separate crescent roll dough. Place an apple wedge on the wide edge of each piece of dough and roll up. Place the dumplings in a 9x13-inch buttered dish. In a saucepan, melt butter with sugar, vanilla and cinnamon over medium heat; stir in SKI. Pour mixture over dumplings. Cover with foil and bake 15 minutes; remove foil and bake 15 minutes longer. Serve with ice cream. Simple and delicious.

What is SKI? It is a citrus soda bottled in our little town that became famous when The Kentucky Headhunters produced a song titled, "Dumas Walker" that featured a slawburger, fries, and a bottle of SKI.

Restaurant Recipe

Baked Tilapia with Shrimp, Tomato, and Mushroom Lemon Cream Sauce

Fish:

1 (6-ounce) tilapia fillet

Drakes Seasoned Flour

4 to 6 ounces (1 to 1½ sticks) butter or extra virgin olive oil

Lightly coat tilapia fillet in seasoned flour. In a 12-inch sauté pan, heat butter. Brown 1 side of the fillet and flip. Place in a 350° oven and bake 7 to 8 minutes.

Sauce:

1 cup heavy whipping cream

2 shrimp, peeled and diced

1 mushroom, diced

¼ medium tomato, diced

1 teaspoon lemon juice

Dash each: seasoned salt, black pepper and Old Bay seasoning

Parsley flakes, optional

In an 8-inch sauté pan over medium heat, combine cream, shrimp, mushroom, tomato, lemon juice and seasonings except parsley. When sauce is just short of boiling, reduce heat and simmer until sauce reduces and becomes thick.

Plate fillet and pour sauce over top. Garnish with parsley flakes, if desired. Yields 1 serving.

Restaurant Recipe

Chasers Restaurant

**110 North Proctor Knott Avenue
Lebanon, KY 40033
270-699-2221**

Nestled in the heart of Kentucky, Chasers is family-owned and is a staple in Lebanon. The small, hometown environment caters to everyone, and the menu offers a vast variety of delicious foods that range from juicy, tender steaks to flavor-filled pastas. Come in and try some the town's favorites—savory baked tilapia, juicy baby back ribs, and succulent made-to-order thick burgers. "Here's to living life to the fullest and always having a reason to celebrate!"

**Monday – Saturday:
4:30 pm to 10:00 pm**

Coon Hunters Cake

2 cups sugar

2 cups flour

2 eggs, beaten

1 tablespoon vanilla

1 (20-ounce) can pineapple chunks, undrained

Combine all ingredients and pour into a 9x13-inch baking pan. Bake at 350° for approximately 25 minutes, or until top springs back when pressed in the center. For best results, frost cake with Cream Cheese Icing while warm.

Cream Cheese Icing:

2 (8-ounce) packages cream cheese, softened

2 cups powdered sugar

1 cup chopped nuts

Combine all ingredients and mix well. Frost warm cake.

Restaurant Recipe

Farmer's Feed Mill

110 Sequoia Drive
Leitchfield, KY 42754
270-230-0027

For more than thirteen years Farmer's Feed Mill Restaurant has been serving quality, home-style food in an atmosphere that you can only get sitting around the table with family. That is exactly what they strive for in Leitchfield, Kentucky. Farmer's Feed Mill offers a unique blend of home-style cooked foods and top-quality, hand-cut chargrilled steaks as well as an extensive menu offering many specialty dishes. So if you are ever passing through town, stop by and find out what happens around their family table.

Monday – Saturday: 7:00 am to 8:00 pm

Mississippi Mud Cake

1 cup butter

½ cup baking cocoa

2 cups sugar

4 eggs at room temperature, slightly beaten

1½ cups self-rising flour

Pinch salt

1½ cups chopped pecans

1½ teaspoon vanilla

1 (16-ounce) bag miniature marshmallows

Melt butter and cocoa together over low heat. Remove from heat and cool slightly. Stir in sugar and beaten eggs; mix thoroughly. Add flour, salt, pecans and vanilla. Spoon batter into greased and floured 9x13-inch pan. Bake at 350° for 35 to 45 minutes. (While cake bakes, prepare frosting.) Sprinkle marshmallows on top of cake and bake about 5 minutes more, until lightly browned and gooey. Cover with chocolate frosting while cake is hot.

Frosting:

2 cups powdered sugar

½ cup whole milk

⅓ cup cocoa

4 tablespoons butter, softened

Combine sugar, milk, cocoa and softened butter. Mix until smooth and spread over hot cake.

Restaurant Recipe

Bluegrass Café

Inside Derby City Antique Mall
3819 Bardstown Road
Louisville, KY 40218
502-459-2320

Locals and visitors alike love the charming and quaint atmosphere of Bluegrass Café where you will enjoy a delicious meal plus the convenience of shopping for antiques at Derby City Antique Mall. Bluegrass Café's unique menu offers traditional, southern food as well as incorporating new ideas. They are open to customers' requests for vegetarian, vegan, gluten-free, and sugar-free dishes for walk-in diners and small formal groups as well as church groups and tour groups. Mr. Joe smokes Boston butt that is delicious with his homemade barbecue sauce. You may also be entertained by the gentle and non-threatening spirits that are said to roam the hallways and the café.

Tuesday – Thursday: 11:00 am to 4:30 pm
Friday: 11:00 am to 3:00 pm
Saturday: 11:00 am to 4:30 pm
Sunday: 12:00 pm to 3:30 pm

Bootleg Bar-B-Q & Catering Co.

9704 Old Bardstown Road • Louisville, KY 40291
502-239-2722 • www.bootlegbbq.com

Bootleg Bar-B-Q, located just three miles south of I-265 on Old Bardstown Road, provides a variety of dine-in or carryout options as well as a full suite of catering services. For more than twenty years Bootleg has established itself as a true Kentucky original with their lean and tender pit-smoked barbeque, made-from-scratch side dishes, desserts, and sauces. The foundations of their signature "Bootleg-style" offerings are rooted in old-fashioned cooking techniques and "from the farm" family recipes handed down through the generations, drawing heavily from Kentucky's rich tradition of smoked and cured meats and home-style country cooking. Locals and travelers alike stop by for generous helpings of down-home hospitality and barbeque that's "So Good It Oughta Be Illegal!"

Sunday – Thursday: 11:00 am to 8:00 pm • Friday & Saturday: 11:00 am to 9:00 pm

Bread Pudding with Honey Bourbon Sauce

Bread Pudding:

¾ pound day-old bread, diced to 1-inch cubes (about 3 to 3½ cups)

½ cup golden raisins

4 tablespoons butter

½ pound brown sugar

1½ teaspoons salt

½ teaspoon allspice

1 tablespoon cinnamon

2 cups milk

½ tablespoon vanilla extract

3 eggs, beaten

Preheat oven to 350°. Place diced bread in a mixing bowl. Soak raisins in warm water to cover. Melt butter, drizzle over bread and toss. Combine sugar, salt, allspice and cinnamon; sprinkle over bread. Drain raisins, add to bread mixture and toss. In a separate bowl, combine milk, vanilla and eggs. Place bread mixture in greased 9x12-inch baking dish. Pour milk mixture over and gently work into bread. When raisins rise, push back down into bread mixture. Bake approximately 1 hour (top should be brown and a toothpick inserted into middle of pudding should come out clean).

Roux:

6 tablespoons butter

½ cup flour

In small skillet, melt butter and whisk in flour until smooth.

Honey Bourbon Sauce:

1 cup honey

½ cup bourbon

3 cups water

½ (16-ounce) box brown sugar

1¼ cups white sugar

½ teaspoon salt

¼ teaspoon vanilla extract

Combine sauce ingredients in a saucepan over medium heat. When sauce comes to boil, slowly whisk in roux until sauce thickens. Dish warm pudding and spoon Honey Bourbon Sauce on top.

Bootleg Bar-B-Q & Catering Co.
Restaurant Recipe

Burgoo Stew

Old-timers say this delicious soup is to be made with venison, rabbit, squirrel, turtle, sheep, a chicken or two—anything unfortunate enough to wander into the crosshairs. This is a more modern recipe for civil folk but still retains the same delicious blend of meat and vegetable flavors.

¾ **pound beef**
¾ **pound pork**
¾ **pound lamb or mutton**
1 **pound chicken**
1 **pound turkey**
Flour to coat meat
½ **cup olive oil**
1 **tablespoon salt**
½ **tablespoon black pepper**
½ **tablespoon red pepper**
3 **tablespoons Kitchen Bouquet**
2 **cups diced potatoes**
2 **cups diced carrots**
1 **cup lima beans**
2 **cups whole-kernel corn**
1 **cup green beans**
2 **cups diced onions**
½ **cup diced green bell peppers**
1 **(14-ounce) can crushed tomatoes**
2 **cloves garlic, crushed**
1 **cup diced or sliced okra**
1 **cup diced celery**
1 **cup minced parsley**

Cut beef, pork and lamb into 1½-inch cubes, making sure all have some fat. Remove skin from fowl and dice. Toss all meat in flour to lightly coat. In a large cast-iron kettle or heavy stockpot, heat olive oil over high heat. Working in batches, brown meat on all sides. When done, drain oil and return meat to pot; cover with water. Add salt, black pepper, red pepper and Kitchen Bouquet; reduce heat to medium and cover stockpot with lid. Cook 2 hours, or until meat is tender. Add potatoes, carrots and lima beans along with additional water to cover. After 10 minutes, add corn, green beans, onions and bell peppers. Reduce heat to low and cook approximately 1 hour. Add tomatoes, garlic, okra and celery. Reduce heat to simmer and cook another hour. Add parsley and cook a half hour longer. Stir often to prevent sticking; add small amounts of water to thin as needed. Finish with additional salt, black and red pepper to taste, if needed.

Bootleg Bar-B-Q & Catering Co.
Restaurant Recipe

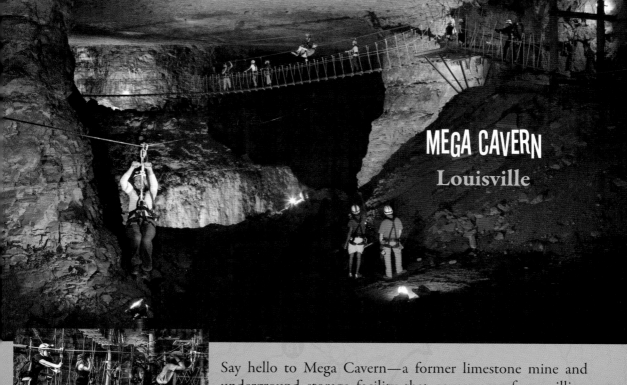

MEGA CAVERN
Louisville

Say hello to Mega Cavern—a former limestone mine and underground storage facility that covers over four million square feet and has been turned into an underground playland. Take the MEGA Tram for an underground tour to see early cavern formations, a worm recycling/tasting room, the early mining operation, and more. MEGA Zips features six underground zip lines that will take you into never before seen sections of the cavern. MEGA Quest is the only fully underground aerial ropes challenge course in the world.

The temperature inside the cavern hovers at a comfortable fifty-eight degrees year round making it the perfect stop on your next trip to Louisville. From mid-November through December you can drive your own car through Mega Cavern to see "Lights Under Louisville," a mile-long trail of blinking reindeer and Nativity scenes in the world's only underground drive-through holiday light show.

1841 Taylor Avenue
Louisville, KY 40213
502-855-6342
www.louisvillemegacavern.com

The Café:
Fresh American Cuisine

712 Brent Street
Louisville, KY 40204
502-589-9191
thecafetogo.com

The Café has gathered legions of loyal fans since 1996 by offering ample portions of fresh, home-cooked food with a Southern accent, served with love in a restored warehouse with a comfortable vintage vibe. Experienced restaurateurs Sal and Cindy Rubino delight in offering one of Louisville's most enjoyable, affordable breakfast and lunchtime dining experiences. Sal is usually "out front" greeting and serving guests, while Cindy has drawn on her decades of cooking experience to develop The Café's unique menu of hearty breakfasts, mouth-watering pastries, satisfying sandwiches, elegant salads, hearty soups, and decadent desserts. Eat at The Café once, and you'll be back.

Monday – Saturday: 7:00 am to 4:00 pm

Strata Alla Cucina

This vegetarian brunch specialty has been popular at The Café for years. Can be made ahead. Serve with a simple fruit salad to complete your Café experience.

4 tablespoons (½ stick) butter

½ cup diced yellow onions

1 cup sliced white mushrooms

½ teaspoon salt

1 teaspoon dried oregano

½ teaspoon white pepper

2 cloves fresh garlic, peeled and minced

1 (6-ounce) bag fresh baby spinach

1 loaf stale French bread, ½-inch slices (discard heel ends)

12 slices (9 ounces) Swiss cheese

½ cup grated Parmesan cheese, divided

10 large eggs

1 quart heavy cream (may substitute 4 cups whole milk)

1 cup whole milk

6 slices fresh tomato

Put rack in middle of oven and preheat to 400°. Melt butter in large sauté pan. Sauté onions and mushrooms with salt, oregano and white pepper for 3 to 5 minutes. Add minced garlic and continue to cook until onions are translucent and mushrooms have rendered most of their liquid, another 4 to 5 minutes. Remove from direct heat and add spinach, stirring to wilt.

Lightly grease a 9x13-inch pan. Loosely cover bottom of pan with slices of bread. (Avoid heel ends or large chunks that will not absorb the egg mixture, as they can cause the strata to be tough.) Spoon vegetable mixture over bread. Cover entire surface with Swiss cheese slices and sprinkle half of the Parmesan cheese (¼ cup) over top.

In separate bowl, whisk together eggs, heavy cream and milk. Pour custard mixture over bread, vegetables and cheese. Cover tightly with foil. (Can stop here and refrigerate 12 to 18 hours; remove from refrigerator for 1 hour before baking so strata gets closer to room temperature.)

Bake 1 hour. Remove from oven and garnish with sliced tomatoes and remaining Parmesan cheese. Return to oven for 5 to 10 minutes, uncovered, to brown slightly. Allow to sit 10 minutes before slicing and serving. Serves 6 to 8.

Restaurant Recipe

Salmon Patties

Patties:

1 (4-pound) can salmon

4 tablespoons ground plain breadcrumbs

1 egg

Salt and pepper to taste

Reserve juice from salmon for pea sauce. Place salmon in a large bowl and discard all bones. Add remaining ingredients and mix well. Form into patties—we make them 2 to 3 ounces and serve 2 patties per order. Deep fry to golden brown. Serve with Pea Sauce, if desired.

Pea Sauce:

Reserved salmon juice

½ quart (2 cups) milk

5 ounces (about 1 cup) peas

4 tablespoons cornstarch

In a saucepan, combine salmon juice, milk and peas. Bring to a boil; add cornstarch mixed with a little water. Stir well; reduce heat to medium. Continue to cook, stirring frequently, until sauce thickens to a gravy-like texture.

Restaurant Recipe

Cottage Inn

570 Eastern Parkway
Louisville, KY 40217
502-637-4325

In 1929, Harvey Board opened the delicatessen at Eastern Parkway and Bradley Avenue that we now know as the Cottage Inn. The Cottage Inn has always been family owned. The menu has been the same for many years for one simple reason—it works. The friendly folks at Cottage Inn have been serving up simple and affordable home food since 1929. It is one of Louisville's oldest eateries in continuous operation.

Monday – Saturday:
10:45 am to 9:00 pm

Bread Pudding

1 loaf plain French bread

2 cups sugar

3 eggs, beaten

1 cup raisins

1 quart milk

2 tablespoons vanilla

⅓ stick butter, melted

Tear bread and place in large bowl. Add sugar, eggs and raisins. In a separate bowl, combine milk with vanilla; add to bread mixture. Using your hands, crush bread until mixed thoroughly. Pour melted butter into a 9x13-inch pan coating bottom. Pour in bread mixture. Bake at 325° until firm, approximately 55 minutes. Cool before serving.

Whiskey Sauce:

½ pound (2 sticks) butter

2 eggs

2 tablespoons water

2 cups sugar

1½ ounces (3 tablespoons) bourbon whiskey

In a small saucepan, melt butter over low heat just until melted. Remove from heat; cool 10 minutes. Beat eggs with water; combine with butter in saucepan. Add sugar; mix well. Cook over medium-low heat, stirring constantly. When sauce begins to boil and sugar is fully dissolved, remove from heat. Whisk in bourbon. Cool 10 minutes; serve over Bread Pudding.

Restaurant Recipe

Joe's OK Bayou

9874 Linn Station Road
Louisville, KY 40223
502-426-1320
www.joesokbayou.com

Joe's OK Bayou has been servin' up the best Cajun food since 1995. From crawdads and gator tail to a bushel of oysters, even the keenest Cajun connoisseur will be delighted in this hidden gem right off the interstate in the suburbs of Louisville. You will feel right at home in "da Bayou" with their wood shack decor, tin roof, and swamp murals. Of course, every year during Mardi Gras season, you can expect beads, King Cake, entertainment, and Hurricanes to all make an appearance during the festivities at Joe's OK Bayou! They pride themselves on great food and friendly service that is "second to none," plus delicious Cajun fare at a terrific value. Whether you dine in, carryout, or have it catered, visit Joe's OK Bayou to enjoy the authentic taste of "da Bayou" today!

Monday – Thursday: 11:00 am to 9:00 pm
Friday: 11:00 am to 10:00 pm
Saturday: Noon to 10:00 pm
Sunday: Noon to 9:00 pm

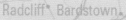

Lilly's Bistro

1147 Bardstown Road
Louisville, KY 40204
502-451-0447
www.lillyslapeche.com
www.facebook.com/lillysbistro
Twitter: @lillysbistro

Are you in the mood for a casual lunch, hand-crafted cocktail, or dinner with friends for special occasion or any occasion? Make your dining destination Lilly's—A Kentucky Bistro. Behind their six-time Beard Award-nominated chef Kathy Cary, they've led the effort to support local farmers by using products grown within a short distance of the restaurant —organic vegetables, free-range beef, Kentucky Proud beef, artisan cheeses, and more. Their mission is to provide an unparalleled dining experience that reflects the original flavors of the Bluegrass state. Make a reservation to dine today. Or join them for one of the many special events, such as wine and cocktail pairings and prix fixe meals.

Tuesday – Saturday,
Lunch: 11:00 am to 3:00 pm
Dinner: 5:00 pm to 10:00 pm

Chicken Pâté of Fresh Goat Cheese & Herbs with Nectarine Salsa

Chicken Pâté:

2 pounds boned, raw chicken breasts

2 eggs

¼ cup fresh dill

¼ cup fresh tarragon

2 teaspoon salt

Dash nutmeg

Dash cayenne

3 cups heavy cream

8 ounces fresh goat cheese, divided

½ cup sun-dried tomatoes, chopped and rehydrated, divided

Oil a pâté or loaf pan and preheat oven to 350°. In a food processor, purée chicken, eggs, dill, tarragon, salt, nutmeg and cayenne till smooth. While processor is running, add heavy cream and blend well. Pour a third of this mixture into the oiled pâté pan. Crumble 4 ounces goat cheese on top and sprinkle with ¼ cup tomatoes. Repeat, and end with last third of chicken mixture. Set pan in a larger pan on oven's middle rack. Pour enough boiling water in larger pan to come half way up sides of pâté pan. Bake 1 hour and 15 minutes, or until a knife inserted into the middle of the pâté comes out clean. Remove and serve in individual slices arranged on a plate with Nectarine Salsa.

Nectarine Salsa:

2 cups sugar

1 cup cider vinegar

1 tablespoon grated ginger

2 cups thinly sliced nectarines

⅓ cup diced red onion

¼ cup chopped cilantro

Heat sugar, vinegar and ginger in a saucepan over medium heat. When sugar dissolves, remove from heat and add nectarines, onion and cilantro. Let cool. Pour around the base of the Chicken Pâté and serve with toast.

Restaurant Recipe

Mark's Feed Store

www.marksfeedstore.com

MIDDLETOWN
11422 Shelbyville Road
Louisville, KY 40243
502-244-0140

DIXIE HIGHWAY
10316 Dixie Highway
Louisville, KY 40272
502-933-7707

HIGHLANDS
1514 Bardstown Road
Louisville, KY 40205
502-458-1570

NEW ALBANY
3827 Charlestown Road
New Albany, IN 47150
812-949-RIBS (7427)

FERN CREEK
6501 Bardstown Road
Louisville, KY 40291
502-442-0808

Mark's Feed Store has been a Louisville tradition since 1988. The concept and dream started in a historic building from 1933 that had once been used as Hancock Feed Store. Mark's Feed Store has since grown to five locations in the greater Louisville area. Mark's cooking style was handed down from a third generation master from eastern Kentucky, and many of the menu items are carefully guarded and trademark secrets. The "feed" is down-home-style BBQ at its finest—tender, hand-pulled pork and chicken with a special tangy sauce; fresh, never frozen, fall-off-the-bone baby back ribs; sweet fried corn on the cob; and Mark's famous buttermilk pie. The company motto is "Friendly Folks Servin' Famous BBQ."

Sunday – Thursday: 11:00 am – 10:00 pm
Friday & Saturday: 11:00 am – 11:00 pm
(9:00 pm at the New Albany location)

BBQ Pork Roll

1 quart coleslaw (cabbage) mix
¼ cup pickle relish
½ tablespoon minced garlic
1 green onion, small dice
½ rib celery, small dice
¼ pound pork, fine dice
¼ cup red barbecue sauce
5 (10-inch) tortillas

Combine all ingredients, except tortillas, in a mixing bowl. Mix well. Place 4 ounces pork mixture onto a tortilla. Fold tortilla over pork mixture from 1 side, then fold both sides over flap, then roll tortilla (make sure it is a round roll). Finished roll is approximately 7 inches long. Dab a small amount of water under fold to seal and put 2 toothpicks lengthwise into tortilla to hold together. Heat oil in a frying pan. Cook approximately 6 minutes, until roll is golden brown. Remove from skillet, remove toothpicks and cut roll in half on a bias cut.

Family Favorite

Pop's Pepper Patch

**425 East Burnett Avenue
Louisville, KY 40217
502-523-6154
www.popspepperpatch.com**

Pop's Pepper Patch has been offering delicious pepper sauces, habagardil pickles, and salsa since 1993. Though they are not a restaurant, a book featuring food would not be complete without some of Pop's Pepper Patch specialties including Chipotle Pepper Sauce and Red Pepper Jelly. The crowd favorite, by far, is Pop's Pepper Patch Habagardil Pickles which are a perfect blend of taste and heat using habanero and de arbol peppers combined with dill and garlic to create the most amazing bread and butter pickles ever. Not your ordinary bread and butter pickle, though, because these pack a kick. They start sweet then give a perfect punch of heat at the end that leave you wanting another . . . and another.

**Available in many stores or online at
www.popspepperpatch.com.
Don't miss out on these unique products
created right here in Louisville, Kentucky.**

Fried Habagardil Pickles

1 egg, beaten

1 cup milk

1 tablespoon Worcestershire sauce

1 teaspoon Pop's Pepper Patch Smoky
Habanero Pepper Sauce to taste

3½ cups plus 1 tablespoon flour

¾ teaspoon salt

¾ teaspoon pepper

1 (16-ounce) jar Pops' Pepper
Patch Habagardil Pickles
(you choose the heat)

Oil for deep frying

Combine egg, milk, Worcestershire, pepper sauce and 1 tablespoon flour; set aside. In a separate bowl, combine 3½ cups flour, salt and pepper, stirring well. Drain entire jar of habagardils. Dip pickles in milk mixture and dredge in flour mixture, repeat process. Deep fry in hot oil (350°) until pickles float to surface and are golden brown. Drain on paper towels.

Restaurant Recipe

Shrimp and Wings in Pop's BangUp Sauce

This recipe makes a lot of wings and shrimp. But be prepared. Every time we have taken this to a party it is the first thing that disappears—every time. They taste almost as good at room temperature as they do hot.

This recipe is very flexible. The magic is in the creamy, spicy sauce. You can bread the wings and shrimp yourself (a recipe follows), or make it easy on yourself and buy prebreaded shrimp (the coconut kind are especially good!). Leave the wings "naked" (unbreaded) or even use store-bought fried "buffalo wings."

Another thing that makes this a great party preparation is that you can make the sauce several days in advance and just keep it in the refrigerator until needed.

Fried Shrimp and Wings:

1½ pounds of the biggest shrimp you can find

2 to 3 pounds of the biggest chicken wings you can find

½ cup oil

1 egg, beaten

1 cup all-purpose flour

½ cup milk

¾ teaspoon seasoning salt

¼ teaspoon salt

Oil (enough for deep frying)

Peel and devein shrimp and set aside. Combine ½ cup oil and egg; beat well. Add remaining ingredients, except oil for frying, and stir until well blended.

Dip shrimp into batter to coat. Drop shrimp into hot oil (350°) and fry 30 to 60 seconds or until golden brown. Remove with slotted spoon; drain on paper towel. Repeat with wings.

Options: Add a ½ teaspoon of baking powder to batter to make a much lighter crust, or use beer instead of milk for a barley flavor.

Pop's BangUp Sauce:

1 cup mayonnaise

8 teaspoons chili garlic sauce (find this in the Chinese section of your grocery or Oriental market)

2 teaspoons sugar

1 teaspoon rice vinegar

4 tablespoons Pops' Smoky Habanero Pepper Sauce (use more or less to taste)

½ cup crushed peanuts, optional

½ cup chopped green onions (only the green part), optional

Mix it all together in a bowl. Pour over the prepared shrimp and chicken wings. Sprinkle peanuts and onions over shrimp and wings, if desired. Eat and Enjoy.

Family Favorite

Coney Sauce

5 pounds ground chuck

1 medium onion, finely diced

1 cup brown sugar

½ cup white sugar

2 cups ketchup

¼ cup yellow mustard

Dash cinnamon

1 tablespoon Worcestershire sauce

Dash allspice

In a large pot, brown meat with onion. Add sugars plus ketchup, mustard, cinnamon, Worcestershire and allspice. Simmer 20 minutes and serve over hot dogs on buns.

Restaurant Recipe

Chandler's

212 Market Street
Maysville, KY 41056
606-564-6385

Chandler's is the place to go in Maysville for delicious food, excellent service, and terrific atmosphere. Specializing in steak and seafood, their diverse menu offers everything from Philly cheese steak sandwich to baked salmon, strawberry chicken salad to Chandler's special Boursin Burger. With excellent sides and desserts handmade from fresh ingredients, you won't be disappointed in the meal at this unique restaurant. The staff is always friendly and helpful for an all-around experience you are guaranteed to enjoy.

Tuesday – Thursday: 11:00 am to 9:00 pm
Friday & Saturday: 11:00 am to 10:00 pm

Cabbage Casserole

1 large head cabbage, cut into 8 wedges

½ cup butter

1 (8-ounce) carton Velveeta (or sharp Cheddar cheese), cubed

1 cup half-and-half or whole milk

Salt to taste

White pepper (so you cannot see specks) to taste

Boil cabbage in water and/or chicken stock until tender; drain and place in casserole dish. While cabbage cooks, melt butter in boiler pan over low heat. Add cheese, half-and-half, salt and pepper. Cook until cheese melts, stirring constantly. Once it is smooth pour over cabbage. Let sit 15 minutes so cheese covers cabbage and has a chance to settle in. Bake at 350° for 15 minutes or until top is bubbly.

Restaurant Recipe

Tomato Soup

1 large onion, finely diced

Olive oil

1 (64-ounce) can whole peeled tomatoes

1 cup sugar

½ teaspoon garlic powder

½ cup heavy cream

In a large stockpot, sauté onion in a small amount of olive oil. Add tomatoes with juice and bring to a boil. Add sugar and garlic powder. Cook about 10 minutes to let flavors marry. Take off heat and run through a blender. Mix until smooth. Add back to pot and add heavy cream just to lighten up the color. Serve.

Restaurant Recipe

Mama Lou's Bar-B-Que

1512 Main Street
Munfordville, KY 42765
270-524-3287

5112 South Jackson Highway
Horse Cave, KY 42749
270-786-4198

Mama Lou's Bar-B-Que is owned by Gerald and Wanda Judd. The Judds met in the restaurant business over thirty-eight years ago and have been cooking ever since. Mama Lou's offers a variety of smoked meats including pulled pork, baby back ribs, and brisket. Not in the mood for barbecue? They also serve burgers, BLT sandwiches, grilled chicken sandwiches, and even fried bologna. There are several great side dishes to choose from including white beans, baked beans, potato salad, and their famous skillet-fried potatoes. The fried cornbread alone is worth the trip! Don't forget to save room for dessert like Mama Lou's own Brown Sugar Pie.

Monday – Friday: 6:00 am to 7:00 pm
Saturday: 10:30 am to 7:00 pm
Sunday: 10:30 am to 4:00 pm

Mama Lou's Brown Sugar Pie

1 cup brown sugar
½ cup flour
Premade 8-inch pie shell
2 cups heavy whipping cream
1 teaspoon vanilla
Sprinkle of cinnamon
½ stick butter, shaved

Mix brown sugar and flour together. Place in bottom of pie shell. In a separate bowl, combine whipping cream and vanilla; pour over brown sugar/flour mixture. Sprinkle top of pie with cinnamon and shaved butter. Bake 1 hour and 10 minutes at 350°.

Restaurant Recipe

Coca-Cola Cake

1 cup Coca-Cola

1 cup buttermilk

2 cups all-purpose flour

¼ cup cocoa

1 teaspoon baking soda

1 cup butter, softened

1¾ cups sugar

2 large eggs, lightly beaten

2 teaspoons vanilla extract

1½ cups miniature marshmallows

Combine cola and buttermilk. In a separate bowl, combine flour, cocoa and baking soda. In a large mixing bowl, beat butter at low speed, gradually adding sugar until blended. Add dry mixture alternately with cola mixture, ending with dry mixture, until well blended. Add eggs and vanilla; beat well. Stir in marshmallows; pour into a greased and floured 9x13-inch pan. Bake at 350° for 30 to 35 minutes. Remove from oven; allow to cool while make frosting.

Frosting:

½ cup Coca-Cola

½ cup butter

3 tablespoons cocoa

1 (16-ounce) package powdered sugar

1 tablespoon vanilla

Boil first 3 ingredients over medium heat until butter melts. Whisk in sugar and vanilla until smooth. Immediately pour over warm cake.

Restaurant Recipe

Earl G Dumplin's

1207 Old Gallatin Road
Scottsville, KY 42164
270-239-3275

Earl G's has been a Scottsville favorite since December 2007. The company was founded by Scottsville native Michael Wood and two former associates, Brent Ramsy and Karl Uebersohn, who all worked in management together at Ryan's Family Steakhouse. The idea was to bring together favorite family recipes and an environment not usually offered in a rural area. You are guaranteed to love the daily specials along with menu favorites like chicken livers and chicken tenders as well as the best catfish around. Earl G Dumplin's is open seven days a week for breakfast lunch and dinner.

Sunday – Thursday: 6:30 am to 9:00 pm
Friday & Saturday: 6:30 am to 10:00 pm

Griddle's Country Cookin'

**360 Old Gallatin Road
Scottsville, KY 42164
270-239-3600**

*"Come Get Ya Some Vittles
at Griddle's"*

Griddle's Country Cookin' is cookin' up all your home-style favorites just like mama cooks. Stop in early for a fresh sausage and egg plate and come back for lunch to have a freshly patted hamburger with delicious onion rings. Looking for something different? Try a daily special for local favorites like fried chicken, salmon patties or meatloaf with pinto beans, mashed potatoes, and turnip greens. Don't forget the cornbread—it's a favorite with Griddle's customers.

**Monday – Saturday: 5:00 am to 9:00 pm
Sunday: 5:00 am to 3:00 pm**

Salmon Patties

**4 pounds salmon, deboned
6 eggs, beaten
1 cup buttermilk
1 cup flour
4 cups cornmeal (or more
for consistency)
Salt and pepper to taste**

Mix all ingredients. (You may need to add up to another cup of cornmeal to get the desired consistency.) Shape mixture into patties about 4 ounces each. Cook in a cast iron skillet with enough oil to cover salmon patties. Cook until brown on both sides, flipping once.

Restaurant Recipe

Baked BBQ Chicken

**16 pieces bone-in raw chicken
8 cups ketchup
½ cup soy sauce
2 (16-ounce) bottles light Karo Syrup
2 tablespoons garlic powder**

Place chicken in a pan. Combine remaining ingredients to make a basting sauce. Baste chicken. Bake at 350° for 20 minutes. Take out and baste again. Cook 20 more minutes. Repeat this process every 20 minutes till chicken is fully cooked, about 1 to 1½ hours.

Restaurant Recipe

Caramel Crusted Vanilla Pudding

Crust:

1 cup light brown sugar

½ cup evaporated milk

1 teaspoon vanilla

1 cup sugar

1 stick butter

½ (11-ounce) box vanilla wafers

Combine crust ingredients, except vanilla wafers, in a medium-sized saucepan. Bring to full rolling boil then boil an additional 1½ minutes. Remove from heat. Spray a 2-quart dish then cover bottom with approximately ½ box vanilla wafers. Pour caramel over wafers and set dish in refrigerator to cool while preparing pudding.

Pudding:

1 (5.1-ounce) box vanilla instant pudding

2½ cups cold milk

1 (8-ounce) container Cool Whip

Mix pudding and milk well then whisk for 2 minutes until pudding is thick. Place pudding in refrigerator until caramel crust is cool. Pour pudding over crust and top with Cool Whip.

Local Favorite

Harper's Catfish

3085 Old Gallatin Road
Scottsville, KY 42164
270-622-7557

Family-owned for more than thirty-five years, Harper's Catfish is the "catfish place" that puts Scottsville on the map. The taste of their hand-breaded catfish and made-from-scratch coleslaw keeps the cars lined up to the road every weekend. Harper's is a simple restaurant with awesome food and has become a family tradition for many people. The restaurant is full of familiar faces, many of which are Harpers themselves, as most of the employees are family and have worked there many years. This tight-knit family business focuses on the comfort food that gives Harper's its special charm. When you visit, you won't leave with a recipe for the slaw, but you will leave with your tummy full and a newfound appreciation for good food.

Wednesday & Thursday:
7:00 am to 9:00 pm
Friday & Saturday: 7:00 am to 10:00 pm
Sunday: 7:00 am to 8:00 pm

Claudia's Tea Room

107 Broadway Street
Sonora, KY 42776
270-949-1897

Claudia's Tea Room provides the perfect blend of ingredients for an exciting and unique culinary retreat. Located next door to the Thurman-Phillips Historical Home in the quiet little community of Sonora (population 500), Claudia's Tea Room provides a truly unique experience. You will relax and sip a cup of one of the many varieties of tea while also enjoying a leisurely nine-course feast of exquisite sweet and savory finger foods from a menu that changes monthly. Teas are served at 1:00 pm and 3:00 pm, by reservation only. Call today to schedule your visit.

By reservation only: call 270-949-1897

Pumpkin Cheese Bites

Graham Cracker Crust:

2 sleeves graham crackers, crushed
½ stick butter, softened
½ cup sugar

Combine all crust ingredients just until they hold together. (Use more crushed crackers, if needed.)

Put mini liners in mini cupcake pan; press crust mix in bottom of each liner.

Filling:

2 (8-ounce) packages cream cheese, softened
½ cup sugar
½ teaspoon vanilla
2 eggs, beaten
1 (15-ounce) can pumpkin purée
Pinch cinnamon
Dash nutmeg

Combine filling ingredients until mixed well. Fill minis and bake at 350° until you can touch top and it bounces, about 20 to 25 minutes.

Restaurant Recipe

BBQ Eggs

12 hard-boiled eggs, peeled
1 bottle Frances BBQ Sauce

Place eggs in sauce and marinate at least 1 week before eating. (Do not refrigerate.)

Restaurant Recipe

Grilled Cabbage

¼ head cabbage
Butter spray
Seasoned salt to taste

Spray cabbage with butter spray and sprinkle with seasoned salt. Wrap in aluminum foil and bake at 400° for 45 minutes or cook on the grill until soft.

Restaurant Recipe

Frances B-B-Que

418 East 4th Street
Tompkinsville, KY 42167
270-487-8550

Kentucky's best barbecue joint, Frances B-B-Que has been in business since 1977. Owners David and Jennifer Arms (Frances' son and daughter-in-law) bought the establishment in 1996 and continue this outstanding restaurant's great-tasting tradition. The house specialty is the pork shoulder which is a tender, tasty, smoky piece of pork heaven. Other local favorites include chicken, brisket, homemade sides, vinegar slaw, potato salad, baked beans, and grilled cabbage. When you visit, be sure to try their unique specialty—BBQ Eggs.

Friday, Saturday, and Sunday:
10:00 am to 8:00 pm

A **Lip-Tinglin'** Trip

Kentucky's best barbecue joints serve up sauce that's worth sticking around for.

R&S BBQ

217 West Second Street
Tompkinsville, KY 42167
270-487-1008

For more than twenty-three years, R&S BBQ has been serving great barbecue and sides. Owner Anita Hamilton-Bartlett and staff work to ensure that everyone who visits leaves feeling like family. And because you always serve the best for your family, at R&S you will enjoy quality Southern barbecue every time. A local favorite is the pork shoulder plus pulled pork and chicken—all served with your choice of sauce. R&S BBQ offers the best barbecue around, a great environment, and reasonable prices all served with a friendly smile and a warm welcome.

Tuesday – Saturday: 10:30 am to 6:30 pm

Vinegar Slaw

1 head cabbage
2 carrots
1 medium onion
1 cup sugar
1 cup cider vinegar
½ cup water
Black pepper to taste

Chop cabbage, carrots and onion. Mix sugar, vinegar, water and black pepper. Taste and adjust to suit your preference. Mix all together and chill before serving.

Restaurant Recipe

THINKSTOCK/ISTOCK/ILYANA VYNOGRADOVA COLLECTION

WORLD'S LARGEST BAT

Louisville

Outside the Louisville Slugger Museum is a six-story, 120-foot-tall baseball bat weighing 68,000 pounds. Interestingly, the bat appears to be leaning against the museum building but is actually completely free standing.

This one-of-a-kind bat guards the entrance to the Louisville Slugger Museum & Factory which showcases the history of the Louisville Slugger and baseball in general. Located in downtown Louisville's "Museum Row," the museum features a mix of hands-on exhibits and memorabilia. You can hold a bat used in an actual game from legends like Mickey Mantle, David Ortiz, Cal Ripken Jr., and more. You can stand behind home plate and experience what it feels like to have a 90-mile per hour fastball flying at you. It's a must see for baseball fans and lovers of American memorabilia.

Louisville Slugger Museum & Factory
800 West Main Street • Louisville, KY 40202
502-588-7228 • www.sluggermuseum.com

While in downtown Louisville, check out another type of World's Largest Bat (the vampire kind)—hanging from the brick exterior of Caufield's Novelty, only 3 blocks away.

Caufield's Novelty
1006 West Main Street • Louisville, KY 40202
502-583-0636, www.caufields.com.

Corn Pudding

5 eggs

⅓ cup melted butter

¼ cup sugar

½ cup milk

4 tablespoons cornstarch

1 (15.25-ounce) can whole-kernel corn, drained

3 (14.75-ounce) cans cream-style corn

Preheat oven to 400°. In a large bowl, beat eggs. Add butter, sugar and milk; mix well. Whisk in cornstarch. Stir in all 4 cans of corn. Pour into a 3-quart greased casserole dish and bake 1 hour, or until set. (May also bake in individual casserole dishes or ramekins.)

Local Favorite

Gooey Bars

1 box yellow cake mix

½ cup melted butter

3 eggs, divided

1 (16-ounce) box powdered sugar

1 (8-ounce) package cream cheese, softened

Combine cake mix, butter and 1 egg; press into a treated 9x13-inch pan. Combine sugar, cream cheese and remaining 2 eggs. Beat with an electric mixer until well mixed, about 5 minutes. Spread in pan over cake mixture. Bake at 325° for 35 to 40 minutes. Cool before cutting into bars.

Local Favorite

Elegant Potatoes

10 medium potatoes, peeled and cubed

1 (8-ounce) carton sour cream

1 (8-ounce) package cream cheese, softened

4 tablespoons butter, plus more for top

½ cup chopped chives

Salt and pepper to taste

Paprika

Boil potatoes in salted water to cover until soft; drain. In a large bowl, beat sour cream and cream cheese together; add hot potatoes and beat until smooth. Add butter, chives, salt and pepper; mix. Pour into a treated 2-quart casserole dish. Dot with butter and sprinkle with paprika. Bake at 350° for 25 minutes. Serves 8 to 10.

Local Favorite

Pasta Salad

2 cups cooked macaroni

1 cup diced cooked chicken

¼ cup chopped celery

1 small onion, chopped

½ green bell pepper, diced

1 (1-ounce) package dry ranch dressing

1 cup mayonnaise

1 teaspoon garlic salt

⅓ cup Italian dressing

Combine all ingredients in a large serving bowl. Chill at least 1 hour or until ready to serve.

Local Favorite

Bluegrass REGION

Carefree Casserole

1 cup minute rice

¼ cup chopped onion

1 tablespoon margarine

1 (10.75-ounce) can condensed cream
of mushroom soup

1¼ cups water

2 cups diced cooked chicken

½ cup cooked English peas

½ cup cooked sliced carrots

½ teaspoon salt

⅛ teaspoon pepper

½ cup grated Cheddar cheese

Place rice in a 1½-quart casserole. In a saucepan, sauté onion in margarine until translucent (do not brown). Blend in cream of mushroom soup and water. Stir in chicken, peas, carrots, salt and pepper. Bring to a boil. Stir into rice in casserole dish. Bake uncovered at 400° for 20 minutes. Cover with cheese and return to oven just until cheese is melted.

Local Favorite

Garrett's Restaurant

**215 North Broadway
Carlisle, KY 40311
859-289-7582
Find us on Facebook**

Garrett's Restaurant is family-run and located on the town square in downtown Carlisle. Owned by George and Becky Garrett, the restaurant has been in the same family for forty-four years. Daily lunch specials offer a variety of home-cooked meals consisting of fried chicken, tenderloin and gravy, country-fried steak, fish, or roast beef. You will love the pies and cobblers which are made fresh daily and include coconut, butterscotch, chocolate, and lemon pies, plus blackberry, apple, cherry, peach, and pecan cobblers.

**Daily: 5:00 am to 2:00 pm
Breakfast served until 11:30 am each day.**

Dabble Cake

1½ cups melted margarine

1 teaspoon baking soda

2 cups sugar

3 cups diced apples

3 eggs, beaten

1 cup walnut pieces

2 tablespoons cinnamon

3 cups flour

1 teaspoon vanilla

½ teaspoon salt

1¼ cups powdered sugar Mix ingredients as listed in 4-quart bowl. Grease and flour an angel food cake pan. Bake at 350° for 50 to 60 minutes or until done. Leave in pan until cooled. Remove from pan and frost.

Caramel Frosting:

1 cup dark brown sugar

1½ sticks margarine

⅓ cup cream or canned milk

1 tablespoon vanilla

Mix all ingredients except powdered sugar in a saucepan. Cook until mixture comes to a hard boil, about 4 minutes. Remove from heat and let cool without stirring. When lukewarm, add powdered sugar; stir until thick enough to spread.

Restaurant Recipe

Welch's Riverside Restaurant

**505 Main Street
Carrollton, KY 41008
502-732-9118**

Welch's Riverside Restaurant is family-owned and family-run and has been in business for more than fifty years. The restaurant offers down-home country-style cooking from a full menu plus daily specials and a full salad bar. With a large dining room overlooking the Ohio River, you are sure to enjoy the view along with the service and your meal. Dine in or carryout are both available—it's your choice; reservations are accepted for parties and large groups.

**Monday – Saturday: 5:00 am to 8:00 pm
Sunday: 6:00 am to 3:00 pm**

Piper's Café

**Hamelin Square
520 West 6th Street
Covington, KY 41011
859-291-7287
www.piperscafe.biz**

At first glance, Piper's Café appears to be an old-fashioned, neighborhood ice cream and snack shop. Piper's is all of that and much more, as it is one of the growing number of upscale carryout restaurants offering fresh, locally-sourced products within a menu that changes regularly. Some fun dishes are always available, like all-beef hot dogs and hamburgers made with grass-fed beef. Available seating is all outdoors, so you can bring your dog to lunch with you.

**Monday – Friday: 8:00 am to 7:00 pm
Saturday & Sunday: 10:00 am to 7:00 pm**

Chicken Sausage Gravy

1 yellow onion, diced
2 cloves garlic, minced
1 tablespoon vegetable oil
1 cup low-sodium chicken stock
1 pound ground chicken
3 cups soy milk
2 Roma tomatoes, finely diced
½ cup loosely packed fresh basil leaves, finely chopped
2 teaspoons ground black pepper
3 to 4 tablespoons cornstarch
2 tablespoons liquid butter alternative
1 teaspoon liquid smoke

In a large saucepan, sauté onion and garlic in vegetable oil until onions are soft. Add chicken stock and ground chicken. Cook until chicken is cooked through, stirring constantly to insure chicken breaks up nicely. Stir in milk, tomatoes, basil and black pepper. Simmer, stirring frequently, until mixture begins to simmer. In a separate cup, combine cornstarch with ¼ cup water until well blended. Slowly stir this slurry into your gravy, stirring constantly and continuing to cook until the desired thickness is reached. Note that you may not need all of the slurry, depending on how thick you like your gravy.

Remove from heat and stir in liquid butter alternative and liquid smoke. Taste and adjust seasonings. Serve over piping hot homemade biscuits!

Restaurant Recipe

Tartar Sauce

4 cups mayonnaise

4 tablespoons pickle relish

4 teaspoons onion powder

1 teaspoon salt

1 teaspoon black pepper

1 tablespoon lemon juice

1 tablespoon fresh minced garlic

Combine all ingredients in a bowl and stir. Refrigerate at least 2 hours before serving with fried catfish or other seafood.

Restaurant Recipe

Catfish Breading

¾ cup flour

2 tablespoons Creole seasoning

Salt and pepper to taste

Add all ingredients in a zip-close bag and shake to mix. When ready to use, add fish 1 piece at a time and toss. Deep-fry in oil at 350° for 4 to 6 minutes. Serve with Miss Mary's Tartar Sauce and enjoy.

Restaurant Recipe

Kattleman's Kreek

1276 US Highway 27 South
Cynthiana, KY 41031
859-234-1133

Kattleman's Kreek, originally opened as a base camp to test market for Miss Mary's foods, has grown in popularity creating its own following as a full-service restaurant. They prepare, from scratch, items that are sold to retail markets throughout the state, utilizing locally grown items as much as possible in all of their recipes. From homemade tartar sauce with locally sourced fresh garlic to breaded and deep-fried catfish, slow smoked BBQ with a homemade sweet sauce that will make your mouth water to frozen jalapeño poppers served up with a sweet chili sauce. Kattleman's Kreek's steaks are locally sourced beef cattle from Harrison County. Stop in and experience local hospitality and try a new dish that may be just a few weeks away from appearing on your local grocery shelf.

Open Daily:
10:30 am to 10:00 pm

Never forget the sweaty stuff!

Matth___

Colonial Cottage Restaurant

3140 Dixie Highway
Erlanger, KY 41018
859-341-4498
thecottagenky.com

During the Great Depression people had to get creative to find work. In 1933, Clara Rich identified a need and addressed it by opening a restaurant near a tobacco warehouse where farmers would bring their crops in for sale. Because those farmers were used to home cooking with fresh products, the Colonial Cottage was founded with that concept in mind and has held true to that course ever since.

Serving mostly a local clientele, "The Cottage" defines comfort and comfort food. Breakfast is served all day and the fried chicken continues to be recognized as the best in the area. A popular regional dish is Goetta and The Cottage sells more than any other restaurant in the state, and the desserts, including meringue pies which are made fresh daily, are excellent. Bring your appetite to Colonial Cottage Restaurant and enjoy what others continue to try to emulate.

Monday – Saturday: 6:30 am to 9:00 pm
Sunday: 7:00 am to 9:00 pm

Goetta Dressing

20 ounces Goetta

2 cups chopped white onion

2 cups chopped celery

½ teaspoon white pepper

½ tablespoon Italian seasoning

1 tablespoon granulated garlic

¼ pound (1 stick) butter or margarine

½ teaspoon sage

½ tablespoon poultry seasoning

7½ ounces (about 4 cups) breadcrumbs

2 to 3 cups water

2 tablespoons turkey base, optional

In a large skillet over medium heat, crumble and brown Goetta. Remove from heat to cool (do not drain). Combine sausage and remaining ingredients in a large mixing bowl adding water and turkey base last. (Use turkey base if you are not going to stuff a turkey.) Stuff mixture into a prepared fresh turkey and bake at 375° about 15 minutes per pound of turkey until bird temperature reads 180°. (If baking dressing in a pan, bake for 1 hour at 375°.) For a 15½ pound turkey, bake turkey covered in a standard oven at 375° for 3 hours. Remove cover and bake an additional hour uncovered. Internal temperature of bird should be 180°. Serves 25.

Restaurant Recipe
Original to The Colonial Cottage

Meatloaf

22 eggs

6 tablespoons salt

1 tablespoon black pepper

1 tablespoon Italian seasoning

¼ cup Worcestershire sauce

2 tablespoons minced garlic

½ tablespoon nutmeg

20 pounds ground beef

1½ quarts diced onions

½ quart diced green peppers

¼ quart diced celery

2 quarts rolled oats

Ketchup

Note: Prepare 1 day prior to use.

Place eggs, salt, black pepper, Italian seasoning, Worcestershire sauce, garlic and nutmeg in the bowl of a stand mixer. Mix well. Remove from stand and add ground beef, onions, peppers, celery and oatmeal; mix by hand. Return to mixer and mix about 2 minutes. Place mixture in small gray bus tub and pat down. Place in refrigerator and store overnight.

Next day, divide into 6 loaves. Place in long 4-inch steam table pans. Rub the tops with ketchup. Cover with foil and bake at 425° for 1½ hours.

Restaurant Recipe

Whoopie Bread

Ruckel's uses this unique recipe instead of traditional hushpuppies with its Friday Fish Fry.

4 cups cornmeal

½ cup self-rising flour

¾ cup sugar

4 tablespoons onion powder

2 tablespoons garlic powder

1 cup diced onions

2½ cups milk

Combine dry ingredients, spices and onions; mix. Stir in milk until well mixed. Spread in a buttered baking sheet and bake at 350° for 25 to 30 minutes. Cut into squares and right before serving place in deep fryer for 45 seconds.

Restaurant Recipe

Ruckel's Restaurant

**192 West Highway 70
Eubank, KY 42567
606-379-6400
www.ruckelsrestaurant.com
and follow us on Facebook**

Inspired by the everyday cooking of the family they grew up with, you'll feel at home savoring a great meal in the casual and relaxed dining room of Ruckel's Restaurant. Experience country cuisine, attentive service, and a friendly atmosphere. The restaurant is kid friendly and offers unique home decor items, fishing, and rocking on the front porch. Visit and see what makes Ruckel's one of the most popular restaurants in town and you are sure to hear, "Welcome to the Family."

7 days a week: 6:00 am to 9:00 pm

Oreo Delight

Layer 1:

4 cups crushed Oreos

1 stick margarine, melted

Place crushed Oreos in bottom of 9x13-inch pan. Dribble margarine over cookies crumbs.

Layer 2:

12 ounces cream cheese, softened

1 (12-ounce) carton Cool Whip

2 cups powdered sugar

1 teaspoon milk

Mix all together until creamy and spread over Oreo crust.

Layer 3:

2 boxes chocolate pudding plus ingredients to prepare per package directions

Prepare chocolate pudding per package directions and spread over the second layer.

Layer 4:

1 (8-ounce) carton Cool Whip

Spread over chocolate pudding.

Layer 5:

Crushed Oreos

Sprinkle top with additional crushed Oreos.

Restaurant Recipe

Ruckel's and Nature Seasoning

2 cups salt

1 cup pepper

½ cup sugar

¼ cup onion powder

4 tablespoons garlic powder

4 tablespoons garlic and herb seasoning

4 tablespoons celery seeds

Mix all ingredients well. Fill a shaker (add rice to absorb moisture). Store remaining seasoning in an airtight container or zip-close bag. Use to season burgers, grilled chicken, pork chops, steaks, home fries, sirloin tips, green beans, etc.

Restaurant Recipe

Candleberry Tearoom and Café

1502 Louisville Road
Frankfort, KY 40601
502-875-0485
www.candleberrytearoom.com

Tradition continued—where elegance meets deliciousness, where taste is a fresh pleasure, and tranquility is in each sip: begin, in Victorian surrounds, to celebrate a day which most days miss.

Tradition continued—contemplate our menu; choose your repast and incredible dessert, for sure! Taste it, really taste it; now, isn't life the better.

Tradition continued—speak with a friend; relish a book; consider, reflect, enjoy; a moment, a linger—your choice, you've really got the time; you just have to take it and claim it your own.

Perfect lunch—its ways and means; its taste, its delightfulness; Candleberry's at lunch.

Tradition continued—once again it's yours!

Tuesday – Friday: 11:00 am to 2:00 pm
Saturdays for High Tea, Reservation Only

Michele's Ham Salad

3 ounces cream cheese, softened
2 tablespoons mayonnaise
1 tablespoon spicy mustard
2 teaspoons dill relish
2 teaspoons sweet relish
¼ teaspoon black pepper
½ teaspoon onion powder
⅛ teaspoon garlic powder
⅓ cup country ham, torn in large pieces
⅔ cup honey ham, torn in large pieces

With an electric mixer, blend cream cheese and mayo well, scraping bowl often. Add remaining ingredients, except ham. Blend well, scraping bowl. Add ham. Blend well until mixture changes consistency (close to the look of a chunky Spam).

Restaurant Recipe

KENTUCKY MILITARY HISTORY MUSEUM
Frankfort

The old Kentucky Arsenal, a looming presence on a hill overlooking the state capitol in Frankfort, houses the Kentucky Military Museum—home to a large collection of Kentucky, Union, and Confederate memorabilia, including identified uniforms, flags, guns, and other equipment. Built in 1850, the building initially did not even have a set of stairs leading to the second floor, but rather an ammunition hoist for moving goods around.

When visiting, don't miss the William Goebel exhibit. Goebel was an American politician who served as the thirty-fourth governor of Kentucky for four days in 1900. Goebel was mortally wounded by an assassin the day before he was sworn in and remains the only state governor in the United States to be assassinated while in office. The 1900 assassination was a political power struggle that almost led to civil war in the state and immediately focused attention on the Arsenal building, where all the military equipment in Kentucky was stored.

125 East Main Street • Frankfort, KY 40601
www.history.ky.gov/portfolio/kentucky-military-history-museum
502-564-3265

The Meeting House Bed & Breakfast, Café and Gift Shop

519 Ann Street
Corner of Ann and Mero Streets
Frankfort, KY 40601
502-226-3226
themeetinghousebandb.com

The Meeting House is a charming 175-year-old Federal home located in the historic district of Frankfort where you will enjoy a little New England-style ambiance while relaxing on the patio among the shade trees. After relaxing you may enjoy a stroll in the beautiful gardens, including two Fairy Gardens. Enjoy a delicious meal in the café or in one of two well-appointed dining rooms where you can chat with owners Gary and Rose Burke while you enjoy a large selection of homemade entrées, sandwiches, and desserts—all cooked by Rose.

SUMMER HOURS
Monday – Friday: 8:30 am to 5:00 pm

Kentucky Burgoo

A regional favorite

2 boneless skinless chicken breasts

3 boneless pork chops

1 pound stew meat

3 onions, diced

1 green bell pepper, diced

1 small turnip, diced

2 (14-ounce) cans crushed tomatoes

1 (10¾-ounce) can tomato purée

1 gallon water

1 (15-ounce) can butter beans

1 cup finely chopped cabbage

1 (8-ounce) package chopped frozen okra, thawed

3 stalks celery, chopped

1 cup whole-kernel corn

1 carrot, shredded

Salt and pepper

4 dashes hot sauce

5 shakes Worcestershire sauce

2 tablespoons sugar

Cooked rice

Put meats, onions, pepper, turnip, tomatoes and tomato purée in a large pot; bring to boil.

Add water and remaining ingredients except rice. Reduce heat to low and simmer 2 hours. Serve over rice. Enjoy.

Restaurant Recipe

The Meeting House Lasagna

2 pounds ground beef

2 onions, diced

2 (15-ounce) cans crushed tomatoes

1 (8-ounce) can tomato sauce

1 (6-ounce) can tomato paste

4 (8-ounce) packages cream cheese, softened

28 ounces sour cream

3 eggs

2 boxes ready-bake lasagna noodles

1 (16-ounce) package shredded Parmesan cheese

1 (16-ounce) package shredded Italian cheese

1 (16-ounce) package shredded sharp Cheddar cheese

In medium saucepan, brown ground beef and onions till well done and meat breaks up. Add tomatoes, tomato sauce and tomato paste. Mix together cream cheese, sour cream and eggs.

Layer in a 9x13-inch casserole dish by covering bottom with sauce. Put a layer of noodles, then a layer of cream cheese mixture and sprinkle a third of each of the shredded cheeses. Repeat the layers 2 more times but end with sauce on top. Bake at 350°, covered, until bubbly.

Restaurant Recipe

FatKats Pizzeria & Restaurant

3073 Paris Pike
Georgetown, KY 40324
502-570-0773
www.fatkatspizzeria.com

The FatKats Experience—Good Times & Great FOOD! FatKats loads their pizza, pastas, salads, subs, and burgers all the way to the edge with homemade freshness and flavor. And, homemade isn't just a catch phrase at FatKats— it's truly the way they do things. You will find homemade items throughout the menu from fresh made dough to hand-rolled appetizers, from fresh-cut vegetables to homemade sauces, and more. FatKats is the two-time winner of Best Pizza Midwest and Best Pizza Central Kentucky, and has been voted the Readers Choice for Best Pizza Georgetown and Best Pizza Central Kentucky. Visit them today and savor the FatKats Experience: award-winning pizza, heavenly subs and burgers, mouth-watering pastas, fresh-cut salads, friendly service, and more!

Sunday – Thursday: 11:00 am to 9:00 pm
Friday & Saturday: 11:00 am to 10:00 pm

Kentucky Hot Brown Pizza

1 teaspoon salted butter
3 tablespoons all-purpose flour
1½ cups milk
½ cup shredded Cheddar cheese plus more for topping
¼ teaspoon salt
¼ teaspoon ground red pepper
Pizza crust of choice
½ cup diced ham or to taste
½ cup diced turkey or to taste
½ cup cooked and crumbled bacon or to taste
1 to 2 tomatoes, sliced

Melt butter in a small saucepan over medium heat; stir in flour. Gradually add milk, whisking until blended. Cook until thick, about 10 minutes, stirring constantly. Remove from heat; add ½ cup cheese, stirring until cheese melts. Stir in salt and red pepper. Spread over your favorite pizza crust. Top with diced ham and turkey. Cover with cheese. Top cheese with bacon and tomato slices. Bake at 375° until cheese is browning and crust is golden brown. Slice, serve and enjoy. One piece will do you.

Restaurant Recipe

Unstuffed Pepper Soup

1½ pounds ground beef

3 large green bell peppers, chopped

1 large onion, chopped

2 (14.5-ounce) cans beef broth

2 (10.75-ounce) cans condensed
tomato soup, undiluted

1 (28-ounce) can crushed tomatoes,
undrained

1 (4-ounce) can mushrooms

1½ cups cooked rice

In a Dutch oven or large saucepan, cook beef, bell peppers and onion over medium heat until meat is no longer pink; drain. Stir in broth, soup, tomatoes and mushrooms; bring to a boil. Reduce heat, cover and simmer at least 30 minutes, stirring occasionally. Add rice and heat through. Serve immediately.

Restaurant Recipe

Fava's Restaurant

**158 East Main Street
Georgetown, KY 40324
502-863-4383**

Fava's, located in historic downtown Georgetown, is owned and operated by a mother (Jeni) and daughter (Sheri) team. Originally from Louisiana, they moved to Kentucky in 1990. Both grew up in the restaurant business in Louisiana, owning a little diner known for its seafood. Fava's is known for the award-winning catfish which you can get any time of day as a sandwich, a po' boy, or a dinner. People also rave about the frickles (fried pickles) and Hot Browns. If you are into heat you need to try the Rings of Fire (fried jalapeños). Another local favorite is the hand-pattied burgers which are great topped with homemade beer cheese. And if you have a sweet tooth, try Jeni's homemade pies which are said to be the best in town.

Monday – Saturday: 6:30 am to 9:00 pm

Lock & Key Café

201 East Main Street
Georgetown, KY 40324
502-867-1972
www.lockandkeycafe.com

If you like great food, you can find it at Lock & Key Café. If you love historic buildings full of charm and character; small, inviting downtowns; and great food that's fresh, homemade, and hot, then Lock & Key is a must see and eat stop. Hot and cold sandwiches, salads, and soups are the main fare, along with a fantastic beverage bar featuring hot and cold espresso specialty drinks, locally roasted coffees, shakes, smoothies, and desserts, all topped off with a big Georgetown smile. Centrally located, locally owned, and easy to find right on the corner of Main and Hamilton, Lock & Key Café has free wireless all the time. For a unique and satisfying dining experience, visit them soon.

Monday – Saturday: 8:00 am to 8:00 pm
Sunday: 10:00 am to 3:00 pm

Lock & Key Café Chicken Salad

We sell pounds and pounds of chicken salad at Lock & Key Café. The following recipe does not have measurements; we mix it up to taste. We don't use a lot of mayonnaise as we believe chicken salad should be about the chicken. Instead, we put more mayonnaise on the bread to make it how the customer likes it.

Chicken breasts
Garlic
Salt
Almond slivers
Mayonnaise
Dried parsley
Celery, chopped
Dried cranberries
Black pepper

Simmer chicken breast on stovetop with garlic and salt for 2 hours, until tender. (Tender, garlic-y chicken is the key.) Remove and cool. Carefully toast almond slivers on baking sheet for 10 minutes at 350°. Place chicken in a large bowl and shred by hand to bite-size pieces. Add mayonnaise, dried parsley, chopped celery, dried cranberries and almonds. Mix well. Add salt and pepper to taste, and adjust any other ingredients to suit your taste. Serve as sandwiches, with crackers, or on a bed of lettuce with choice of dressing.

Restaurant Recipe

Lemon Pie

2 lemons
3 tablespoons flour
3 tablespoons cornstarch
1⅔ cups sugar
5 egg yolks
2 tablespoons butter
2 cups hot water
1 (8-inch) pie shell

Grate zest off each lemon being careful not to go deeper than the yellow of the lemon rind. Squeeze juice from lemons and add to zest. Set aside. In a saucepan, mix flour, cornstarch and sugar. Add egg yolks and butter. Add hot water. Cook over medium heat, stirring constantly, until mixture gets very thick. Remove from heat; add lemon juice and zest. Mix well. Quickly pour mixture into pie shell. (If it is not done quickly it will turn color sitting in the pan.) Top with a meringue and bake at 350° until brown on top, 5 to 10 minutes.

Restaurant Recipe

Sam's Restaurant

1973 Lexington Road
Georgetown, KY 40324
502-863-5872

Sam's Truck Stop was established around 1952 by Sam Leverton. Open twenty-four hours, the business thrived on serving truck drivers a good, home-cooked Kentucky meal. Over the years, Sam's Truck Stop has evolved into a family restaurant and is better known as Sam's Restaurant. After over forty years, a new Sam's was built next to the original building. Proprietors Kevin and Cindy Tipton have been running Sam's for over twenty years, and today Sam's Restaurant is well known for its quality, well-proportioned Kentucky home-cooked meals using original recipes. Local favorites are the homemade cream pies and salad dressings. For a family-friendly atmosphere and Kentucky home cooking, Sam's Restaurant is the place to go.

Monday – Saturday: 9:00 am to 10:00 pm
Sunday: 8:00 am to 8:00 pm

News Café and Antiques • Goldstar B&B

94 Main Street • Gratz, KY 40359
502-484-2919 • www.newandvintage.com

News Café and Antiques and Gold Star Bed & Breakfast is located on the bank of the Kentucky River in Gratz. This area of the state is known as the Golden Triangle, between Cincinnati, Lexington, and Louisville. The cafe, antique store, and bed-and-breakfast are located at the crossroads of Kentucky Highway 22 and Kentucky Highway 355 and 22 miles from the historic capital city of Frankfort. The Gratz Bridge is the only river crossing for forty miles.

Monday & Tuesday: 9:00 am – 7:00 pm
Wednesday: 9:00 am to 2:00 pm
Thursday – Saturday: 9:00 am to 7:00 pm

New's Café features home-cooked food and desserts plus sandwiches and carryout. The daily menu features country ham, brown and white beans, fried potatoes, fried cabbage, and cornbread plus homemade chili and soups. A local favorite is the homemade Banana Caramel Cake.

The 1,000-square-foot **Antiques store** is housed in an old pharmacy built in 1906

with the original herringbone floor, an old tin ceiling and a 24 by 6-foot mural. A country grocery is located in the same building so you can get what you need all in one place. As they say, "We have everything from A to Z—antiques to apple pie, zucchini to Zest soap."

Fried Cabbage

½ pound bacon

1 head cabbage

Salt and pepper

Fry bacon in a large skillet. Remove bacon and reserve for another use leaving drippings in skillet. Wash cabbage then core and shred. Add to skillet and season to taste with salt and pepper. Cook over medium heat, turning frequently, until golden brown, about 10 to 15 minutes.

Restaurant Recipe

Old Timey Green Beans

1 gallon fresh-cut green beans

1 (2-inch x 2-inch) chunk of jowl bacon or salt pork

½ teaspoon salt or to taste

In a large pot, combine beans with 2 gallons water. Bring to a rapid boil over high heat. Reduce heat to medium and keep at a boil for 1 hour adding water as needed. Drain water. Cover with fresh water; add salt pork and salt. Simmer 2 hours or until most of the liquid is gone. Watch closely to prevent burning. Taste and add more salt if needed.

Restaurant Recipe

Goldstar Bed & Breakfast is a four-room suite with two bedrooms and a modern kitchen and bath. The original hardwood floors and period furniture are accented with prints of the nearby Kentucky River (which is about 300 feet from the building) by artist Paul Sawyier. Sawyier was a Kentuckian who lived in Frankfort and painted many local river scenes in the early 1900's.

Cloud's Country Cooking

1028 North College Street
Harrodsburg, KY 40330
859-734-0086
www.cloudscountrycooking.com

Cloud's Country Cooking is family-owned and operated since 2005 by Keith and Cathy Cloud. If you are looking for good food and a pleasant dining experience, Cloud's is the place. The menu reflects home cooking—some selections even carry family names. If you have special requests, Keith and Cathy will try to meet them. Like sweets? All desserts are made on site by Cathy and make a perfect finish to any meal. The atmosphere is relaxing, the service friendly, making this the perfect place to sit back and enjoy a great meal with great friends. Keith and Cathy are focused on good food, family, and friendship. Stop in, try it out, and meet the family—they will probably be the ones waiting on you.

Monday – Saturday: 11:00 am to 8:00 pm
Sunday: 11:00 am to 3:00 pm

Cloud's Country Cooking Stack Pie

Pies:

6 eggs, beaten

1 cup evaporated milk

3 cups sugar

¾ cup (1½ sticks) margarine

1 teaspoon vanilla

4 pie crusts, unbaked

Preheat oven to 350°. Combine eggs, evaporated milk, sugar and margarine in a saucepan over medium heat. Cook, stirring constantly, until hot. Remove from heat and stir in vanilla.

We use premade frozen pie crusts in aluminum foil pie pans. You can use your own favorite pie crust recipe; make enough for 4 pies. Choose 1 pie crust to use as the bottom, and leave as is. Carefully trim back edges of other 3 crusts, so there is no crust overhanging on the pan (only bottom and sides). Fill each pie crust with equal amounts filling. Bake 30 minutes. Cool.

Caramel Icing:

2 cups brown sugar

1 cup (2 sticks) margarine

½ cup milk

1 teaspoon vanilla

Powdered sugar

In a saucepan over medium-high heat, bring brown sugar, margarine and milk just to a boil, stirring. Remove from heat; stir in vanilla. Beat in enough powdered sugar to get an icing consistency.

Carefully remove cooled pies from pans. Spread icing over bottom pie (the 1 with intact edges). Place second pie on top of first, and top with icing. Then stack the third and fourth the same way, topping each with icing. Ice top and sides like a cake. Slice into wedges to serve.

Serves 20.

Restaurant Recipe

The Treehouse Café & Bakery

**426 Main Street
Hazard, KY 41701
606-487-1931
www.treehouse.vpweb.com
www.facebook.com/
TreehouseCafeBakery**

Treehouse Café & Bakery is a hub of activity for local arts and music. The relaxed, café atmosphere and commitment to offering the highest quality food at affordable prices make them a local favorite for entertainment, conversation, and laughter. Works by local artists are displayed throughout the building and weekend music ranges from bluegrass and folk to blues, rap, and punk. Cupcakes and sweets are a staple of the appeal of the warm and welcoming community fostered at The Treehouse, and the level of quality of food offered is nearly impossible to beat in the area.

**Monday – Thursday: 11:00 am to 5:00 pm
Friday: 11:00 am to 9:00 pm
Saturday: 3 pm to 9 pm
(Expanded Summer Hours)**

Italian Panini

This makes a great tasting and very filling sandwich. It's quick and easy to make for get-togethers, sleepovers, parties, or as a nice mid-day meal.

Cuban bun or hoagie roll

**Italian dressing to taste
(we prefer creamy Italian)**

2 ounces thinly sliced ham

1 to 1½ ounces salami or pepperoni

1 lettuce leaf

1 tomato slice

2 to 3 slices Swiss cheese

2 to 3 slices cooked bacon

Butter

If necessary, slice bun and open. Spread dressing on top and bottom buns. Layer ham and pepperoni over bottom bun. Place lettuce and tomato over meat. On top bun, layer cheese and bacon. Close sandwich and butter outside of bun—top and bottom. Place entire sandwich in a Foreman grill on 350° for 6 to 10 minutes.

Restaurant Recipe

MOTHER GOOSE HOUSE
Hazard

What has egg-shaped windows, light-up automobile headlights for eyes, and sits on a large oval stone "nest"? It's the Mother Goose House, of course.

Born from the imagination of George Stacy, a Hazard native, it was built on a shoestring budget almost completely by hand between 1935 and 1940. The Mother Goose House is a monument to Stacy's creativity, and Stacy's wife, Ollie has been quoted as saying that her husband just came home one day with the idea of building the house after hunting geese. The exterior "nest" of the Mother Goose house is made of sandstone gathered from creeks in the area. The goose's body is the roof of the house, and the head is about fifteen feet high.

Originally the residence of Stacy and his family, the building consists of three bedrooms, a living room, kitchen, bath, dining room, and a large family room. The building has since served as a grocery store and a bed-and-breakfast, and is once again someone's home.

The Mother Goose House has been a Hazard/Perry County landmark for more than seventy years. Don't miss it when you are in the area.

2906 North Main Street
Hazard, KY 41701
(Currently a private residence so only
available for viewing as you drive by)

Hill of Beans BBQ

1040 Bypass South 127
Lawrenceburg, KY 40342
502-839-5936

SECOND LOCATION:
101 Man O War Drive
Danville, KY 40422

Hill of Beans BBQ is an outside grilling, smoking, and barbequing restaurant serving pulled pork that is smoked for fifteen hours. Local favorites include the baby back ribs, beef brisket, grilled chicken breast, rib eye sandwiches, and the famous wood-grilled six-ounce Bubba Burger. Hill of Beans offers plate lunches, everything from meatloaf and pork chops to roast beef, glazed hams, and broaster chicken combos. The most requested dish is Hill of Bean's hot baked potato salad which is smothered with cheese, bacon, and the secret ingredient. Stop by Hill of Beans and enjoy authentic barbecue and meet the famous "Bubba" grill master.

Monday – Saturday: 6:00 am to 10:00 pm

Hot Baked Potato Salad

This is a "teaser" for the real thing . . . we couldn't get grill master Bubba to give away the complete recipe.

Boiled potatoes, diced and sliced
Sour cream
Salad dressing
Vinegar
Hard-boiled eggs
Sugar
Bacon bits
Cheddar cheese
The secret ingredient

Combine all ingredients then top with additional cheese and a sprinkle of bacon bits. Heat in convection oven at 350° for 30 minutes or until warm throughout. This mouth-watering, belly-filling dish is our most requested food dish.

Restaurant Recipe

Best Chocolate Cake Ever

4 ounces semisweet chocolate

⅓ cup margarine

1¾ cups all-purpose flour

1½ cups sugar

1½ teaspoons baking soda

1 teaspoon salt

1½ cups dairy sour cream

2 eggs

1 teaspoon vanilla

Melt chocolate with margarine; set aside to cool. Preheat oven to 350°. Combine dry ingredients. With an electric mixer, beat sour cream, eggs and vanilla in a large mixing bowl. Add dry ingredients and beat until smooth. Add melted chocolate and beat 3 minutes at medium speed. Pour into a 9x13-inch greased pan. Bake 25 to 30 minutes. Cool.

Caramel Frosting:

⅓ cup butter

1 cup packed brown sugar

⅓ cup evaporated milk

2 ounces semisweet chocolate

2 cups powdered sugar

1 teaspoon vanilla

Melt butter in a small saucepan over low heat. Add brown sugar and evaporated milk. Bring to boil, stirring frequently. Remove from heat; add chocolate and stir until melted. Cool to room temperature in a bowl. Beat in powdered sugar and vanilla. Spread over cooled cake.

Local Favorite

Billy's Bar-B-Q

**101 Cochran Road
Lexington, KY 40502
859-269-9593
www.billysbarbq.com**

If you are looking for good old country barbeque cooking, Billy's Bar-B-Q is the place to be. In 1978, Billy Parham and Bob Stubblefield decided it was time to introduce the people of Lexington to the taste of real pit barbecue. Coming from West Kentucky, where barbecue is king, they knew just how to do it. Specializing in the best ribs, pulled pork, beef brisket, mutton, and chicken wings around, Billy's also offers delicious, lip-smacking sides, including their world-famous Kentucky Burgoo. For more than thirty-five years, Bill's Bar-B-Q has honed their skills to perfection. You'll agree when you taste their outstanding barbecue.

**Monday – Thursday: 11:00 am to 9:00 pm
Friday & Saturday: 11:00 am to 10:00 pm
Sunday: 11:30 am to 8:00 pm**

Doodles Breakfast and Lunch

262 North Limestone
Lexington, KY 40507
859-317-8507
www.doodlesrestaurant.com

Chef Brian says, "Here at Doodles we strive to be a different type of restaurant. Every day we work very hard to find the freshest sources for our food. We try to know where it was grown and how it was grown. The majority of our food is sourced within fifty miles of our location or grown ourselves without pesticides or GMO crops, thus allowing us to serve the freshest and most wholesome food in Lexington!" For the freshest, most delicious food around, try Doodles for breakfast and for lunch.

Tuesday – Sunday: 8:00 am to 2:00 pm

Huevos Rancheros

1 cup medium-diced yellow onions
1 tablespoon minced garlic
1 pound dried black beans
1 jalapeño
2 fresh cayenne peppers
Kosher salt, to taste
1 teaspoon cumin
1½ teaspoons oregano
1 bay leaf
1 (16-ounce) bottle beer
Oil for frying
Flour tortillas
Fried eggs

Sauté onions until soft, about 5 minutes. Add garlic; sauté until fragrant, about 1 minute. Put into large pot along with beans, whole peppers, salt, cumin, oregano and bay leaf. Add beer; add water to cover at least 3 times the volume of beans. Soak overnight. Bring to a boil, lower heat, cover and simmer until done.

Pour oil to ½ inch deep in an 8-inch pan and heat to 350°. Fry tortilla shells until they begin to color, remove from oil and drain on paper towel. Place tortillas on plate, top with beans and fried eggs. Garnish with your choice of toppings.

Restaurant Recipe

Toffee Bread Pudding

Day old bread, diced ½-inch cubes
¼ cup hot water
¼ cup brown sugar
4 tablespoons crumbled toffee
2 eggs
1 cup milk
¼ cup sugar
¼ teaspoon vanilla
¼ teaspoon cinnamon
¼ teaspoon salt
4 tablespoons heavy cream
Caramel sauce

Coat inside of 4 soufflé cups with butter and then with granulated sugar. Fill cups one half to two thirds with bread cubes. Lightly press down. Mix hot water and brown sugar. Pour 1 ounce into each cup coating bread.

Sprinkle 1 tablespoon crumbled toffee into each soufflé cup. Mix eggs, milk, sugar, vanilla, cinnamon and salt together. Pour 6 ounces into each soufflé cup. Bake in a 350° oven for 25 to 30 minutes or until a knife inserted in center comes out of clean. Break open the top with a spoon and pour in 1 tablespoon heavy cream. Top with caramel sauce and serve slightly hot. Makes 4 servings.

Restaurant Recipe

RJ Corman Lexington Dinner Train

150 Oliver Lewis Way
Lexington, KY 40509
866-801-3463
www.lexingtondinnertrain.com

Experience a unique view of Kentucky's horse country with the RJ Corman Lexington Dinner Train. Travel through some of the world's most famous horse farms while seated in a meticulously restored dining car. All tables are set with crisp linens, china, and crystal and offer a picture window so you won't miss any of the action. The award-winning culinary team prepares your gourmet meal on board while an attentive waitstaff serves you with a generous side of Southern hospitality.

Limestone Blue

133 North Limestone
Lexington, KY 40507
859-749-5670

Limestone Blue offers creative local food and creative local art in a community-based environment. Their refreshingly creative menu offers unique sandwiches and sides made with quality, fresh ingredients. A local favorite is the daily mac and cheese specials—everyone loves the Buffalo Mac and Cheese.

This locally driven and inspired eatery plus beer and wine bar is also a nonprofit art gallery (100 percent of the sale goes to the artist). Serving as a hangout spot for locals, Limestone Blue welcomes visitors as they support local artists, local food, and the growing downtown community of Lexington.

Monday – Friday:
10:30 am to 10:00 pm
Saturday: 9:00 am to 10:00 pm

Superfood Salad

This salad is packed with powerful vitamins, nutrients, and protein. It can easily be made vegan by not adding the crumbled feta and substituting raw sugar for honey.

Salad:

3 cups chopped fresh kale

½ Granny Smith apple, sliced

½ avocado, sliced

⅓ cup cooked red quinoa

¼ cup crumbled feta cheese

¼ cup walnuts

Lay kale leaves out flat on a plate. Alternate apple slices and avocado slices in a circle over kale. Top with quinoa, feta and walnuts. Makes 1 salad (8 servings). Serve with Dressing recipe below.

Dressing:

1 cup olive oil

1 cup balsamic vinegar

2 tablespoons honey

1 tablespoon Dijon mustard

Whisk all ingredients together until well blended. Serve 2 ounces dressing with each salad. Makes enough for 8 servings.

Restaurant Recipe

Broccoli Salad

This sweet and savory side dish is a hit at any picnic, barbecue, or family event.

Salad:

1 small red onion, diced

1 cup raisins

1 cup walnuts

1 cup bacon crumbles

2 broccoli heads, chopped

Combine onion, raisins, walnuts and bacon in a large bowl. Add Dressing and stir until well coated. Add broccoli and mix with hands until all ingredients are distributed evenly. Makes 8 (1-cup) servings.

Dressing:

¾ cup mayonnaise

¼ cup sugar

1½ tablespoons white wine vinegar

Mix mayonnaise, sugar, and white wine vinegar.

Restaurant Recipe

Meadowthorpe Café

1415 Leestown Road
Lexington, KY 40511
859-258-2222

This family-friendly, sit-down restaurant offers many deals your taste buds will beg for and your wallet will love—the most popular of which are the outstanding burgers. Local

favorites are the Meadowthorpe and Spalding burgers. The Meadowthorpe is a seven-ounce patty with all of the traditional dressings, an over-hard egg, and bacon on a grilled bun. The Spalding is a six-ounce patty with an over-hard egg, cheese, and bacon all on a Spalding doughnut from the legendary Spalding Bakery. Daily lunch specials are available during the week and feature delicious signature dishes you simply won't find anywhere else. These favorites are influenced by family traditions and are based on time-honored recipes that were handed down through generations. Drop by to gobble up some mouth-watering fried catfish, delicious meatloaf, or some fantastic fried chicken.

Come early for delectable breakfast deals. We hope to see you there.

Monday & Tuesday: 8:00 am to 2:00 pm
Wednesday – Saturday:
8:00 am to 3:00 pm
Sunday Brunch: 8:00 am to 2:00 pm

Meatloaf for 20

10 pounds ground beef
1 pound onions, diced small
2 cups Worcestershire sauce
12 eggs
4 cups rolled oats
4 tablespoons salt
4 tablespoons pepper
2 tablespoons granulated garlic
2 cups brown sugar

Blend meat in mixer on low speed. Add onions, Worcestershire and eggs; blend well. Add dry ingredients and blend 1 minute on low. Set mixer speed to 2 and blend 1 minute. Treat a 2-inch hotel pan with nonstick spray. Place mixture in pan and press to edges. Press well to remove all air pockets. Center should be slightly lower than edges. Cover with foil. Bake 1 hour at 350°. Remove cooked meatloaf; drain grease. Slice ½-inch short-ways across pan. Cover with meatloaf topping and bake an additional 15 minutes.

Meatloaf Topping:

1 (114-ounce) can ketchup
1 pound brown sugar

Mix together in tall square container with snap lid.

Restaurant Recipe

Ranch Dressing

1 cup mayonnaise
½ cup sour cream
1 clove garlic, finely minced
¼ cup minced parsley
2 tablespoons minced fresh dill
1 tablespoon minced fresh chives
1 teaspoon Worcestershire sauce
¼ teaspoon salt
½ teaspoon ground black pepper
½ teaspoon white vinegar
¼ teaspoon paprika
⅛ teaspoon cayenne pepper
¼ cup buttermilk or more as needed for desired consistency

In a bowl, combine mayonnaise, sour cream, garlic, parsley, dill, chives, Worcestershire sauce, salt, black pepper, vinegar, paprika and cayenne. Add buttermilk until you get the consistency you desire. This recipe doubles well. For a ranch dip, increase the sour cream and reduce the buttermilk.

Restaurant Recipe

Parkette Drive-In Restaurant

1230 East New Circle Road
Lexington, KY 40505
859-254-8723
www.theparkette.com
www.facebook.com/parkette.fans

Randy and Jeff Kaplan became the fifth owners of Parkette Drive-In Restaurant in March 2009. Parkette was founded in 1951 by Joe Smiley who was a pioneer in the industry. Beginning with walk-up service, Parkette went to carhop service later in the 1950's and added indoor seating in the 1970's. The menu still features Joe's original recipes, including Fried Chicken, Hot Dog Chili Sauce, and the Famous Kentucky Poor Boy Burger—voted #5 in Food Network's *Diners, Drive-Ins & Dives* Top 10 of All Time in December 2013. The same month, Parkette's Hot Brown Burger was featured on the *Rachel Ray Show*. In addition, the restaurant was featured on Food Network's *Diners, Drive-Ins, & Dives* hosted by Guy Fieri in September 2010. In 2013, Parkette Drive-In Restaurant added a full-service, retro 1950's garage-style dining room adding ninety seats.

Monday – Wednesday: 11:00 am to 8:30 pm
Thursday: 11:00 am to 9:30 pm
Friday & Saturday: 11:00 am to 10:00 pm

The Famous
Kentucky Poor Boy

This double-decker, quarter-pound cheeseburger was created in the mid-1940's. The Kentucky Poor Boy may be the second double-decker ever created in the US. The first was at Bob's Big Boy in Los Angeles in 1937.

**Fresh 3-part bun
(top, bottom and middle)**

Parkette sauce (fortified mayonnaise)

Shredded lettuce

**2 (⅛-pound) 80/20 beef patties,
seasoned and cooked to
desired doneness**

Mustard

1 slice American cheese

1 thick slice onion

1 slice tomato

Pickles

Build the burger in the following order: Bottom bun, Parkette sauce, lettuce, burger patty, middle bun, mustard, cheese, burger patty, onion, tomato, pickles, top bun.

Restaurant Recipe

Hot Brown Burger

Baked Potato Wedges with Honey Dijon Yogurt Sauce

3 tablespoons vegetable oil, divided

4 medium potatoes, scrubbed

2 teaspoons cayenne pepper

1 teaspoon ground black pepper

1 teaspoon cumin powder, optional

1 teaspoon garlic salt (or salt)

Place 2 tablespoons oil in a baking tray and place in oven set to 425°; allow oil to heat while preparing potatoes. Cut each potato into 8 wedges, lengthwise. (Potatoes may be prepared skin-on or peeled.) Combine seasonings and 1 tablespoon oil in a large bowl. Toss wedges in spiced oil so that each wedge is lightly coated (work in batches if necessary). Carefully remove baking tray from oven; place wedges in hot oil. Return to oven to roast 30 to 35 minutes or until done (crispy on the outside; tender on the inside). Serve hot with Honey Dijon Yogurt Sauce for dipping.

Honey Dijon Yogurt Sauce:

½ cup lowfat, plain Greek yogurt

2 tablespoons Dijon mustard

1 tablespoon honey

Salt and pepper to taste

Mix well and serve with Baked Potato Wedges.

Local Favorite

THINKSTOCK/ ISTOCK/ OLGAMILTSOVA

Kentucky Chess Pie

1 cup sugar

¾ cup packed light brown sugar

1 tablespoon cornmeal

5 eggs

⅓ cup whipping cream

1 tablespoon cider vinegar

1 teaspoon vanilla extract

½ cup melted butter

1 (9-inch) pie shell, unbaked

Combine sugar, brown sugar and cornmeal. Beat in eggs 1 at a time. Stir in whipping cream, cider vinegar, vanilla extract and melted butter. Pour into unbaked pie shell. Bake at 400° for 10 minutes. Lower heat to 325° and continue baking 45 minutes longer.

Local Favorite

Benedictine Spread

A perfect appetizer for a tea party, Mother's Day luncheon, summer party, and more.

1 large cucumber, peeled

½ to 1 small onion, quartered

1 (8-ounce) package cream cheese, softened

1 tablespoon mayonnaise

½ teaspoon salt

Dash hot pepper sauce

1 drop green food coloring

2 (16-ounce) packages white bread, crust removed

Slice cucumber in half lengthwise, and remove seeds with a small spoon. Place in a food processor and pulse about 5 times, until minced. Place into a small glass mixing bowl. Pulse onion in food processor until finely chopped. Add onion to cucumber. Add cream cheese and mayonnaise; mix well by hand. Stir in salt, hot sauce and food coloring. Spread between 2 pieces of white bread; cut each into 4 triangles using a serrated knife. Makes about 96 small sandwiches.

Local Favorite

Winchell's Restaurant

348 Southland Drive • Lexington, KY 40503
859-278-9424 • www.winchellsrestaurant.com

Winchell's is a unique restaurant that everyone will love. Serving breakfast, lunch, and dinner every day, there isn't a meal they don't have covered. Owners Abe and Graham are trained chefs who brought their love of great food back to Lexington to share it with their hometown. Add that Winchell's has thirty flat screen TVs, a full bar, friendly staff, and focuses on local products, and you have a backyard recipe for the perfect restaurant.

Monday – Sunday: 8:00 am to 1:00 am

Kentucky Hot Brown (top): *Classic Kentucky dish with toast points, shaved country ham and turkey breast, topped with Mornay cheese sauce and baked in the oven until bubbly and golden brown. Finished with sliced tomato, bacon, and Parmesan cheese on top.*

Fried Shrimp Platter (center): *10 hand breaded and deep-fried tiger shrimp, served with hand cut fries, house made creamy coleslaw, and homemade cocktail sauce*

Winchell's Reuben: *Grilled rye bread with homemade 1000 island dressing, shaved corned beef, and house made vinegar coleslaw. Baked in the oven, with melted Swiss cheese.*

SUPER-SIZED DIXIE CUP
Lexington

Thirsty? If you are thinking a cute Dixie cup of water will never be enough to quench your thirst, think again. Outside the Georgia Pacific plant (which used to be the Dixie Cup Corporation) is a water tower that looks like this great American icon. The Dixie Cup Water Tower was built in 1958 very soon after the opening of the Dixie Cup Corporation there.

Built as a giant beacon of corporate branding, the tower has out-survived the original business . . . barely, it seems, and thanks to its close proximity to the airport. As the story goes, Georgia Pacific had plans to dismantle the water tower but was ordered by the city to leave it because the airport uses the extra-large Dixie Cup as a point of reference.

So, the giant Dixie Cup survives. When visiting Lexington, be sure to drive by . . . if you are thirsty enough to handle it.

Dixie Cup Water Tower
on the grounds of
Georgia Pacific
(closed property; viewable
from the road)
451 Harbinson Road
Lexington, KY 40511

York St. Café

738 York Street
Newport, KY 41071
859-261-9675
www.yorkstonline.com

The historic York St. Café, once home to a pharmacy built in the 1880's, has been re-imagined into a retro 1950's decor restaurant voted Best First Date Restaurant. The menu features many lunch and dinner choices—from vegan and gluten free to traditional steak and chicken dishes. A local favorite is the Amish Chicken. Desserts, including Butter Rum Pecan Pudding Cake, are made from scratch. York St. has two upper levels, a night club on the second floor and an art gallery on the third floor. Stop by to see all they have to offer.

LUNCH
Tuesday – Saturday: 11:00 am to 5:00 pm

DINNER
Tuesday – Thursday: 5:00 pm to 10:00 pm
Friday & Saturday: 5:00 pm to 11:00 pm

MERCANTILE HOURS
Wednesday – Saturday: Noon to 3:00 pm
and 6:00 pm to 9:00 pm

Amish Chicken

Hard Cider Sauce:

**1 (12-ounce) bottle Wood Chuck
Hard Cider**

1 pint heavy cream

1 tablespoon chicken soup base

Salt and pepper

Bring cider to a boil and reduce by half.
Add heavy cream and chicken base and
bring to a boil. Reduce heat to a simmer
and cook 10 minutes. Season with salt
and pepper.

Stuffing:

**1 pound applewood smoked bacon,
chopped**

1 medium white onion, diced small

8 ounces Gorgonzola, crumbled

Cook bacon till crisp; remove to a paper
towel to drain retaining drippings in
skillet. Sauté onion in bacon drippings
until soft; cool. Add cheese.

Chicken:

**4 (10-ounce) fresh airline Amish
chicken breasts**

Salt and pepper to taste

Make slit on side of chicken breasts and
use fingers to make a pocket. Fill with
stuffing using about a quarter for each
breast. Season with salt and pepper.

Brown in oiled oven-safe pans till
golden brown. (Don't crowd the skillet,
better to use 2 skillets unless you have a
big one.) Put skillets in oven and bake
at 400° about 30 minutes or until
internal temperature reaches 165°.
Remove chicken to serving plates.

Pour off excessive oil from hot pan. Pour
Hard Cider Sauce in hot skillet and
reduce while scraping off any yummy
chicken bits, then pour over breasts.

Restaurant Recipe

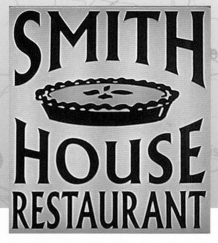

1640 Highway 22 East
Owenton, KY 40359
502-484-2636
www.facebook.com/smithhouse2013

Since 1968, the Smith House has been providing quality, country cooking to generations of families from Owen County, Kentucky and from around the world. Specialties include pulled pork, beef brisket, and baby back ribs—all hickory smoked on-site—along with the famous Willie Whopper Double Cheeseburger. A local favorite is their made-from-scratch Smith House pies. Homemade is the key word when discussing the delicious food at the Smith House. Generations of families have grown up eating there. When you are in town, join them for a great down-home experience.

Monday, Tuesday, Thursday & Friday:
11:00 am to 8:00 pm
Saturday: 11:00 am to 8:00 pm
Sunday: 11:00 am to 3:00 pm

Snowy White Mashed Potatoes

5 cups prepared mashed potatoes
1 (8-ounce) package cream cheese, softened
1 (8-ounce) carton sour cream
4 tablespoons butter, melted
Black pepper to taste

Mix potatoes, cream cheese and sour cream together with an electric mixer to a smooth consistency. Pour into a 3-quart baking dish. Top with butter and pepper. Bake at 350° for 40 minutes.

Restaurant Recipe

Tomato Bisque

1 (106-ounce) can diced tomatoes

2 large yellow onions, chopped

4 tablespoon butter

3 heaping tablespoons chicken base

3 heaping tablespoons dried dill weed

1 quart heavy whipping cream

Purée tomatoes, with juice, in blender until smooth. Pour into a large stockpot. Sauté onions in butter until translucent; add to tomatoes. Bring bisque to a boil; add chicken base and dill weed. Remove from heat and add cream. Purée soup until almost smooth. Serve in a soup cup or a wide rimmed bowl.

Restaurant Recipe

Spoonbread

4½ cups water

4½ cups milk

3 cups white, self-rising cornmeal

9 eggs, well beaten

2 tablespoons real unsalted butter

Preheat a greased 11x17-inch casserole dish in a 350° oven. Scald water and milk. Add cornmeal and mix well. Fold in beaten eggs and mix well. Stir in butter until melted. Pour into preheated pan and bake until mixture rises and a knife comes out clean.

Restaurant Recipe

Hanger's Restaurant

**2187 Lexington Road
Richmond, KY 40475
859-353-5588
www.hangersrestaurant.com**

Rebecca G. Chenault says, "As a young lady, I lived in a beautiful home named White Pines, originally owned by the Hangers—a family very prominent in Richmond's colorful history. Noted for their philanthropy, horsemanship and love of community, they donated the stately home 'Arlington' to Eastern Kentucky University, which played a major role in the creation of the University of Kentucky Medical Center. Living in White Pines left me with a real connection to the name Hanger. It's my wish that this restaurant honors the history of that name as well as embracing the future so that Hanger's becomes a place where you feel at home to 'hang out' with us and call it your own."

Tuesday – Saturday: 4:00 pm to Closing

The Paddy Wagon Irish Pub

150 East Main Street • Richmond, KY 40475
859-625-1054 • www.richmondpaddywagon.com

Founded in 2004 by Eastern Kentucky University Professors Chuck Fields and Greg Ferrell, The Paddy Wagon Irish Pub has become a mainstay in the downtown Richmond restaurant and pub scene. Voted The Best Bar and The Best Music Venue by the *Eastern Progress* newspaper for the past five years, a night at the Pub is indeed a unique experience. With over one hundred beers (forty on draught) from more than twenty countries, one of the finest selections of Irish whiskey in the region, and food that is first-rate pub fare, the diverse clientele always finds something to suit their tastes.

Monday – Saturday: 11:00 am to 1:00 am

Guinness® Braised Corned Beef and Cabbage

This recipe is one of the tastiest and most appealing we have found and is offered on special occasions —St. Patrick's Day, University Homecoming and Graduation, and more—throughout the year. Enjoy.

4 to 5 pound corned beef brisket

1 cup brown sugar

1 tablespoon caraway seeds

¼ teaspoon ground cinnamon

⅛ teaspoon ground cloves

¼ teaspoon ground allspice

1½ pints Guinness® Stout

½ quart vegetable broth

1 small onion, minced

2 garlic cloves, minced

1 medium carrot, minced

1 celery stalk, minced

1 tablespoon black peppercorns

1 bay leaf

2 pounds carrots, peeled and cut into 3-inch pieces

8 to 10 small red potatoes, washed and halved

1 large sweet onion, peeled and quartered

1 head cabbage, cut into wedges, rinsed well

Don't skip this step, it's very important: rinse corned beef under cold water, and pat dry. Mix brown sugar with caraway seeds, cinnamon, cloves and allspice; rub into brisket, coating both sides thoroughly.

Place brisket on meat rack in a large Dutch oven or covered roasting pan with a cover, GENTLY pouring Guinness over meat, making sure brown sugar/spice mixture gets moist but stays in place. Add vegetable broth, minced onion, garlic, minced carrot, celery, peppercorns and bay leaf. Bake at 350° for 2½ to 3 hours. During last hour of roasting, carefully turn brisket and add remaining carrots, potatoes and sweet onion.

When potatoes are done, add cabbage wedges; cook about 15 minutes more or until cabbage is tender. Remove meat from Dutch oven and set aside for about 15 minutes before slicing. Drain off the Guinness broth and bring to a boil in a saucepan until reduced by about half. Whisk in a little cornstarch to thicken it, if necessary.

Slice corned beef across the grain and serve with the vegetables and the sauce on the side. Serves 12 to 15.

Restaurant Recipe

RT's Bar & Grill

1013 Center Drive, Suite A
Richmond, KY 40475
859-626-5628
www.rtsbarandgrill.com
www.facebook.com/RTscafe

RT's is an upbeat bar & grill with great food and great people. They pride themselves on being a local place where they will know your name by your second visit. Their menu offers a little bit of everything and on the weekends they offer homemade dinner specials— everything from Chicken and Dumplings to BBQ Pulled Pork smoked right on the back patio. They have a lot of entertainment as well—live music on the weekends, billiards, corn-hole, and ping-pong, just to name a few. So come check them out and you'll be saying, "RT's Please!"

Monday – Thursday: 3:00 pm to 1:00 am
Friday & Saturday: 11:00 am to 1:00 am
Sunday: 1:00 pm to 9:00 pm

RT's Cheesy Mac 'N' Pepp

1 (16-ounce) package elbow macaroni

1 tablespoon butter

1 teaspoon Dijon mustard

2 teaspoons minced garlic

1½ tablespoons flour

2½ cups milk

6 ounces cream cheese, cubed

½ cup Parmesan cheese

¾ cup shredded Cheddar cheese
plus more for topping

1 tablespoon dried basil

1 cup chopped tomatoes

1 cup chopped pepperoni

Cook noodles according to package instructions to al dente. Melt butter in a large saucepan. Stir in mustard, garlic and flour to make a roux. Cook about 5 minutes to a nice golden brown color. Gradually add milk, whisking constantly, to avoid burning. Lower heat and simmer about 2 minutes or until consistency of heavy cream. Remove from heat; add cream cheese, Parmesan cheese and ¾ cup Cheddar cheese. Stir until melted. Add basil.

Return to low heat; add cooked noodles, tomatoes and pepperoni. Cook an additional 3 to 5 minutes, just until heated through. Transfer to a 9x13-inch glass baking dish. Top with additional shredded Cheddar cheese to taste.

Topping:

1 cup breadcrumbs

1 tablespoon melted butter

1 teaspoon dried thyme

1 teaspoon garlic powder

½ teaspoon dried basil

½ teaspoon dried oregano

Combine Topping ingredients and sprinkle over casserole. Broil about 5 minutes or just until topping is lightly browned.

Restaurant Recipe

Clear Creek Market

865 Clear Creek Road
Salt Lick, KY 40371
606-683-2170

Clear Creek Market is located in the Daniel Boone National Forest in Bath County, Kentucky. It offers big city taste combined with country hospitality. Homemade pies are a specialty and the burgers are thick, juicy, and delicious. Breakfast is served all day, and the menu also offers a wide variety of food including seafood, steak, soups, biscuit and gravy, omelets, and much more. Clear Creek Market is located next to the White Sulphur OHV trails, White Sulphur Horse Camp, horse trails, and Cave Run Lake so be sure to stop in for some outstanding food and service while you are in the area.

Sunday – Thursday: 7:00 am to 8:00 pm
Friday & Saturday: 7:00 am to 9:00 pm

Homemade Beer Cheese

1 (16-ounce) package Velveeta, room temperature

1 (16-ounce) package shredded sharp Cheddar cheese, room temperature

2½ tablespoons hot sauce

2½ tablespoons Worcestershire sauce

1 teaspoon garlic powder

1½ teaspoons garlic salt

1 teaspoon cayenne pepper

1 (12-ounce) can flat beer

¾ cup Hellmann's mayonnaise

It is important for cheese to be at room temperature. In a food processor, add cheese, hot sauce, Worcestershire and spices; process. Add beer slowly; process. Add mayonnaise; process. Taste and adjust hot sauce and other seasonings if needed.

Restaurant Recipe

Dorothy Sparrow's Chess Pie

3 eggs

1 stick butter, melted

1½ cups sugar

½ cup buttermilk

1 teaspoon vanilla

1 unbaked pie shell

Blend eggs, butter, sugar, buttermilk and vanilla in a blender for 10 minutes. Pour into an unbaked pie shell. Bake at 375° for 45 minutes. Cool and serve.

Restaurant Recipe

Family Affair Restaurant & Catering

5509 Louisville Road
Salvisa, KY 40372
859 865-4096
www.facebook.com/
familyaffairsalvisa

Family Affair Restaurant & Catering was established in 1991 in Salvisa by Dorothy Sparrow and three of her children, Shirley, Judie, and Kent. After Dorothy's passing all four of her children made their way to the restaurant to keep it running like their Mama would have wanted. Every day you can find something good to eat off the buffet or made to order from the grill. Many say it's just like eating at home—except you don't have to do the dishes. From pot roast to fried chicken to catfish, you can find it at Family Affair. Catering is available.

Monday – Thursday: 11:00 am to 8:00 pm
Friday: 11:00 am to 9:00 pm
Saturday: 9:00 am to 9:00 pm
Sunday: 11:30 am to 2:30 pm

Bell House Restaurant

721 Main Street • Shelbyville, KY 40065

502-437-5678 • www.bellhouserestaurant.com

Bell House Restaurant, set in a beautiful historic home built in 1902, was completely renovated by the Andriot family in 2007. Its peachy-pink exterior, showcasing its traditional charm, adorns historic downtown Shelbyville, and its beautiful interior with its welcoming atmosphere is full of delicious food and happy customers.

Executive Chef Tracy Gibson brings unique flavors to a well-balanced menu with luncheon favorites such as Chicken Salad, Goat Cheese Salad, and Asiago Turkey Flat. Popular dinner specialities include Crispy Rosemary Chicken, Pork Scaloppini, and Cedar Plank Salmon.

A visit to downtown Shelbyville would not be complete without a dining experience at Bell House Restaurant!

Lunch, Monday – Saturday: 11:00 am to 2:30 pm
Dinner, Friday & Saturday: 5:00 pm to 9:00 pm

Crispy Rosemary Chicken with a Lemon Rosemary Sauce

Rosemary Breading:

1½ cups panko breadcrumbs

½ cup grated Parmesan cheese

1 tablespoon roughly chopped fresh rosemary

1 teaspoon salt

¼ teaspoon black pepper

Mix all breading ingredients in a shallow dish.

Lemon Rosemary Sauce:

1 cup heavy cream

½ cup chicken stock

½ cup white wine, preferably Chardonnay

1 lemon, zested and juiced

1 tablespoon butter, melted

1 tablespoon flour

1 sprig rosemary, lightly chopped

Salt and pepper, to taste

In a small saucepan, reduce cream to ½ cup over low heat. Add in stock, wine and lemon juice. Reduce to 1 cup. In another pan, make a roux with butter and flour. Whisk roux into lemon sauce. Add in rosemary, lemon zest, salt and pepper. Adjust with additional lemon juice as desired.

Chicken:

3 tablespoons olive oil

4 (6-ounce) boneless, skinless chicken breasts

2 eggs, beaten

3 tablespoons water

Heat sauté pan over medium to medium-high heat. Add 3 tablespoons olive oil. Dip chicken breast in beaten egg and water mixture. Coat in Rosemary Breading. Fry in olive oil until golden brown on both sides and fully cooked.

Plate chicken and lightly spoon Lemon Rosemary Sauce on top.

Garnish:

Lemon slice

Sprig rosemary

Garnish with lemon slice and rosemary sprig. Serves 4.

Chef Tracy Gibson
Bell House Restaurant
Restaurant Recipe

Ken-Tex Bar-B-Q

1163 Mount Eden Road
Shelbyville, KY 40065
502-633-2463
www.kentexbbq.com

Ken-Tex Bar-B-Q, family-owned since 1986, is known for its Texas-style, mouth-watering beef brisket and savory Kentucky-style pulled pork cooked slowly over a hickory fired pit. Their burgoo, Longhorn Stew, is a customer favorite. On Friday nights, the special—smoked salmon—brings in hungry patrons from miles away. Ryan Price, son and manager, has been working at Ken-Tex since 1987.

Sunday –Thursday: 11:00 am to 8:00 pm
Friday & Saturday: 11:00 am to 9:00 pm

Salmon Sauce

2 cups (1 pound) butter
4 cups (32 ounces) olive oil
8 cups (64 ounces) water
8 tablespoons (4 ounces) lemon juice
1¼ cup (10 ounces) Italian dressing
6 tablespoons (3 ounces) liquid Dales Steak Seasoning
¾ cup apple cider vinegar
1¼ cup (10 ounces) Ken-Tex seasoning

Melt butter in a saucepan. Add remaining ingredients. Simmer and stir until well-combined. Serve over grilled salmon.

Restaurant Recipe

Coleslaw

2 heads cabbage, shredded
1 (10-ounce) bag shredded carrots
½ red bell pepper, diced
1 green bell pepper, diced

Combine slaw ingredients in a bowl.

Dressing:

6 ounces (scant cup) sugar
6 tablespoons apple cider vinegar
Pinch celery seed
4 cups mayonnaise
Salt and pepper to taste

Mix dressing ingredients together in a bowl. Combine with slaw and serve.

Restaurant Recipe

Smithfield Milling Co. Fried Cornbread

2 cups self-rising cornmeal

2 cups milk

2 eggs

½ cup melted shortening

Oil for cooking

Mix meal, milk, eggs and melted shortening. Batter will be thin. Drop onto hot oiled griddle using a large spoon. Cook until browned on each side, turning once.

Restaurant Recipe

Chilled Pickled Beets

2 (15-ounce) cans whole beets

1½ cups vinegar

2 cups sugar

Dash ground cloves

Drain beets, reserving liquid from 1 can. Mix reserved liquid, vinegar and sugar in saucepan. Sprinkle cloves on top. Place saucepan on stove over medium heat for 10 minutes, or until sugar is well-dissolved. Stir and pour over drained beets. Chill until thoroughly cooled. Very nice served in a cut-glass bowl with a slotted spoon. Serves 4 to 6.

Restaurant Recipe

Our Best Restaurant

5728 Smithfield Road
Smithfield, KY 40068
502-845-7682
www.ourbestrestaurant.com

Do you want that feeling that you've just come home to Sunday dinner? Then a visit to Our Best is a must. A love of the old Smithfield Mill is the reason the Way family has served homemade dishes for more than twenty-two years showcasing the cornmeal and flour once produced there. Fried cornbread, fried green tomatoes, bean soup, pork chops, and fried chicken are local favorites. And everyone loves the homemade desserts. Once you visit, you'll want to come back. *Louisville Courier-Journal* columnist Byron Crawford stated, "Where there is a will or a mill, there is a way and a WAY." Their success proves it.

Tuesday – Sunday: 11:00 am to 8:00 pm

Hog Wild Pig Crazy Bar-BQ

Love the Taste, Taste the Love

401 Love's Drive • Sparta, KY 41083
859-935-2045
www.hogwildpigcrazybbq.com

Hog Wild Pig Crazy Bar-BQ . . . Love the Taste, Taste the Love. At Hog Wild, they smoke the meats daily . . . everything from pulled pork to brisket and ribs to chicken and sausage. When it's time to eat, you can choose from three mouth-watering sauces. If that's not enough, the homemade sides are delicious and made fresh daily. Enjoy a large selection of drinks, beer, and wine coolers with your meal. Dine inside, outside under the big red umbrellas, or carry it out. Owner Jane Searcy says, "I grew up on a farm where we had our own garden and raised our own meats. I learned to cook country and am proud of it. My goal is having good, home-cooked food every day. My husband and I are both Kansas City Barbecue Judges." Try Hog Wild Pig Crazy Bar-BQ today—it's something to squeal about.

Monday – Saturday: 10:30 am to 9:00 pm
Sunday: 12:00 pm to 8:00 pm
Winter: Close 1 hour earlier

Cheeseburger Soup

½ pound ground beef

¾ cup chopped onions

¾ cup shredded carrots

¾ cup diced celery

1 teaspoon dried basil

1 teaspoon dried parsley

4 tablespoons butter or margarine, divided

3 cups chicken broth

4 cups diced potatoes

¼ cup flour

8 ounces Velveeta cheese, cubed

¾ teaspoon salt

¼ teaspoon pepper

1 cup sour cream, optional

In a 4-quart saucepan, brown beef; drain and set aside. Sauté onions, carrots, celery, basil and parsley in 1 tablespoon butter until tender. Add broth, potatoes and beef. Bring to a boil. Cover and simmer 10 minutes until potatoes are tender. Melt remaining 3 tablespoons butter; add flour and stir. Add enough water to this paste so it will pour. Add to soup and boil 2 minutes. Reduce heat to low. Add cheese, salt and pepper. Cook until cheese melts; remove from heat. Add sour cream, if desired.

Restaurant Recipe

Buffalo Chicken Dip

2 (8-ounce) packages cream cheese, softened

2 (12-ounce) cans chicken, shredded

Frank's Red Hot Sauce to taste

½ (12-ounce) jar ranch or blue cheese dressing

1 (16-ounce) package shredded Cheddar cheese

Spread cream cheese in bottom of a 9x13-inch casserole dish. Layer chicken over cream cheese. Top with hot sauce to taste then ranch or blue cheese dressing. Cover with shredded cheese. Bake at 325° until cheese is melted and dip is heated through. Delicious served with nacho chips.

Restaurant Recipe

Kentucky Depot Restaurant

119 Metker Trail
Stanford, KY 40484
606-365-8040

Kentucky Depot Restaurant is a landmark to folks in Lincoln and surrounding counties. Born from Gladys' love of people and Danny's appetite for her down-home cooking, the restaurant was started August 1991 in the small railroad community of McKinney. Danny and Gladys come from a long line of railroaders, so the railroad theme was a natural for the restaurant. Home-cooked food, Southern hospitality, and friendly staff are just a few reasons Kentucky Depot has been featured in *Southern Living*, *The New York Times* and *Best of the Midwest*. Be sure to try their famous Brown Sugar Pie. If you enjoy being around a loving family atmosphere where the faces never change, Kentucky Depot Restaurant is the place to visit.

Monday – Thursday: 11:00 am to 8:00 pm
Friday & Saturday: 11:00 am to 8:30 pm
Sunday: 11:00 am to 6:30 pm

Brown Sugar Pie

1 cup brown sugar
¼ cup self-rising flour
1 (12-ounce) can evaporated milk
3 eggs, separated (reserve whites for meringue)
¼ cup butter
1 tablespoon Karo syrup
1 (9-inch) baked pie shell

In a saucepan, mix together brown sugar and flour; add just enough evaporated milk to moisten. Add egg yolks and cream well. Add remaining evaporated milk, butter and Karo syrup. Cook over medium heat until thick. Pour into baked pie shell.

Never Fail Meringue:

1 tablespoon cornstarch
8 tablespoons sugar, divided
½ cup water
1 teaspoon vanilla
Reserved 3 egg whites, beaten to a stiff peak

Combine cornstarch, 2 tablespoons sugar and water in a small saucepan. Cook until clear and thick. Remove from heat and add remaining 6 tablespoons sugar and vanilla into hot mixture; mix well. By hand, stir in beaten egg whites. Spread over top of pie and bake at 350° until browned on top.

Restaurant Recipe

Addie's Restaurant at The Woodford Inn

140 Park Street
Versailles, KY 40383
859-873-5600
www.AddiesKY.com
www.TheWoodfordInn.com
Facebook:
Addies and The Woodford Inn

Addie's Restaurant & Bourbon Bar, located on the first floor of the historic Woodford Inn, is open to inn guests and the public for lunch and dinner seven nights a week and for breakfast on Saturdays and Sundays. Serving a variety of southern dishes such as Kentucky's famous Hot Brown, Shrimp and Grits, Citrus Glazed Pork Chop, Bourbon Maple Glazed Salmon, and much more, the lunch menu and bourbon bar menu is offered all day. Visit www.addiesky.com to view their full menu featuring cuisine and desserts that are all homemade in house. Addie's offers on- and off-site catering and will help with any special event you might have. For your enjoyment, they also offer a beautiful dining porch and an outside patio.

Monday – Thursday: 11:00 am to 9:00 pm
Friday: 11:00 am to 10:00 pm
Saturday: 8:00 am to 10:00 pm
Sunday: 8:00 am to 8:00 pm

Stuffed Banana Peppers

16 large banana peppers
2 (8-ounce) packages cream cheese, softened
2 cups shredded mozzarella cheese
5 jalapeños, seeded and small diced
16 egg roll wrappers
Oil for frying

Cut ends off banana peppers, and slice down the middle but not all the way through. Deseed. Mix cream cheese, mozzarella and jalapeños. Stuff each banana pepper with cheese mixture and wrap with egg roll wrapper. Fry until golden brown and serve with your choice of dipping sauce.

Restaurant Recipe

The Glitz

4205 Fords Mill Road
Versailles, KY 40383
859-873-6956
www.irishacresgallery.com
Facebook:
The Glitz at Irish Acres Gallery

The Glitz Restaurant is located in Irish Acres Gallery in "Nonesuch, KY." The meticulously renovated 1930's schoolhouse is brimming over with European and American antiques, collectibles, international giftware, and exclusive boutique items. After browsing the gallery, venture to the lower level where a fairytale setting and gracious staff await you. Begin your three course luncheon with a flute of spiced apple refresher, followed by an appetizer, entrée with accompaniments, and dessert. Try the famous "Nonesuch Kiss" for dessert. The recipes, always prepared with local fresh ingredients, have been developed by and served at The Glitz since 1988.

Tuesday – Saturday: 11:00 am to 1:30 pm
St. Patrick's Day through
the end of December

Gingered Melon Soup

A refreshing purée of fresh cantaloupe with a hint of ginger.

¼ cup minced crystallized ginger
1½ cups orange juice
2 tablespoons freshly squeezed
lemon juice
¾ cup sugar
3 large cantaloupes
1½ cups sour cream
Blueberries and mint sprigs for garnish

Cook ginger, orange juice, lemon juice and sugar in a saucepan over low heat until it begins to simmer. Let cool.

Remove and discard seeds from cantaloupe. Cut flesh into chunks, and put into an electric juicer. Remove pulp from juicer (reserve juice) and combine with sour cream and orange juice mixture in a food processor. Process until smooth. Pour into a large bowl; add melon juice and whisk to blend.

Chill several hours. Serve in small bowls garnished with a couple of blueberries and a sprig of mint. Makes 12 servings.

Restaurant Recipe

Pineapple Tarts with Coconut Ice Cream

Coconut Ice Cream:

4 cups whole milk

2 cups heavy cream

1 cup sugar

7 egg yolks

2 (15-ounce) cans Coco Lopez cream of coconut

Bring milk, cream and sugar to a boil in a heavy saucepan over medium heat. In the top of a double boiler set over simmering water, whisk egg yolks and cream of coconut. Pour a little of the hot milk mixture into the egg yolks (to temper) and whisk to combine. Add the rest of the hot milk mixture gradually. Cook, whisking occasionally, until mixture thickens enough to coat the back of a spoon. Strain through a fine mesh strainer into a bowl. Chill for a couple of hours. Pour mixture into an ice cream freezer and freeze according to manufacturer's instructions.

The Nonesuch Kiss

Pineapple Tarts:

2 sheets frozen puff pastry, thawed slightly

1 large pineapple

½ cup (1 stick) butter

1 cup sugar

½ cup pineapple juice, divided

¼ cup dark rum

¾ cup chopped macadamia nuts, toasted

Set puff pastry on a lightly floured surface. Cut into 8 (4-inch) rounds. Arrange on a parchment-lined baking sheet. Top with a sheet of parchment paper. Place another baking sheet over the second parchment. Bake in a preheated 350° oven for 15 minutes. Remove top baking sheet and parchment and bake 10 minutes longer or until browned. Keep warm.

Peel pineapple, cut out eyes and core (reserve juice as you cut pineapple). Cut into rings. Melt butter in a large skillet; add sugar. Bring to a simmer. Add pineapple and sauté until golden on each side. Add about half the pineapple juice; lower heat if pan becomes too dry or sticky. Pour rum and remaining pineapple juice into skillet. Keep warm.

Divide pastry rounds among 8 plates. Top each with a ring of pineapple. Place a scoop of Coconut Ice Cream in the pineapple ring. Drizzle with pan juices and sprinkle with macadamia nuts. Makes 8 servings.

Restaurant Recipe

Madison's on Main

**110 South Main Street
Versailles, KY 40383
859-873-3000
www.facebook.com/
MadisonsLunchBox**

Located in downtown Versailles, Madison's on Main is locally owned and operated by family and friends who are natives to Woodford County. Serving breakfast every day plus excellent lunch specials, Madison's is already a favorite of locals and is sure to become your favorite, too. Their goal is to provide you with a family-friendly atmosphere, excellent service, and good, homemade food and delicious desserts that will make you want to come back for more.

**Tuesday – Saturday: 7:00 am to 2:00 pm
Sunday: 8:00 am to 2:00 pm**

Andrea's Chili

**1 pound ground beef
1 tablespoon minced garlic
4 to 5 tablespoons chili powder
Dash onion powder
Dash black pepper
¼ cup V8 juice
1 (15.5 ounce) can Brooks chili beans**

Brown ground beef in a large pot over medium heat; drain grease. Add garlic, chili powder, onion powder and pepper; stir. Stir in V8 and beans. Cook over medium heat 15 to 20 minutes.

Restaurant Recipe

Family's Chicken & Dumplings

1 chicken, cut-up

4 cups self-rising flour

4 eggs

Large spoon of lard

Cook chicken with 3 quarts water in a large stockpot over medium-high heat about 45 minutes or until done. Remove chicken from broth; set chicken aside to cool and remove broth from heat. Combine flour, eggs and lard; add 2 cups cold water to make a soft dough. Place on a floured surface and knead until stiff. Roll dough to about ½ inch thick. Let dough rest 15 to 20 minutes. While resting, pick chicken from bones.

Bring broth to a medium-high boil. Cut dough into 3x1-inch strips; drop into boiling broth. Reduce heat to medium-low and cook 10 to 15 minutes. Add chicken. Serve hot.

Restaurant Recipe

Family's Main Street Café

104 North Main Street
Walton, KY 41094
859-485-6520

Family-owned and operated, Family's Main Street Café is a down-home country-cooking restaurant with a friendly atmosphere. You come as a stranger and leave as a friend. Founded February 2001 by their loving GiGi, the restaurant was named Family's because from day one, patrons were treated like family and served food Family's would be proud to serve their own family. Beginning with a small building seating just forty-five people, this outstanding restaurant has expanded to a bigger building that allows seating for eighty-five people. Be sure to stop at Family's Main Street Café to experience the friendly service and good, home-cooked meals.

Monday – Saturday: 6:00 am to 8:00 pm
Sunday: 7:00 am to 7:00 pm

Jewell's on Main

100 East Main Street
Warsaw, KY 41095
859-567-1793
www.jewellsonmain.com

Jewell's on Main is a casual dining restaurant along the Ohio River. The unique dining experience and great food guarantee you will enjoy your visit. Jewell's on Main serves delicious dishes that represent Kentucky regional cuisine with a splash of southern brought back from the owner's travels. Bring the family, have dinner with a friend, or enjoy a night out with that someone special while enjoying anything from meatloaf or orange bourbon salmon to shrimp and grits. Be sure to visit Jewell's on Main; you won't be disappointed.

Tuesday – Thursday: 11:00 am to 9:00 pm
Friday: 11:00 am to 10:00 pm
Saturday: Noon to 10:00 pm

Bourbon Glazed Meatloaf

5 pounds ground beef
1 red bell pepper, diced
1 small yellow onion, diced
10 eggs
½ cup A-1 steak sauce
½ cup Heinz 57 steak sauce
½ cup ketchup
¼ cup Worcestershire sauce
½ cup brown sugar
1 tablespoon each: granulated garlic, salt and pepper
1½ quarts coarse breadcrumbs

Preheat oven to 350°. Combine all ingredients, except breadcrumbs, and mix thoroughly. Add breadcrumbs and mix until distributed. Spray a jumbo-sized muffin pan with nonstick vegetable spray. Place 1 cup mixture in each jumbo muffin mold. Bake at 350° for 30 minutes or until juices run clear. Cool, then cut each meatloaf in half and grill until internal temperature is 165°. Serve immediately topped with Bourbon Glaze.

Bourbon Glaze:

1 cup ketchup
1 cup prepared bourbon sauce (Minors Bourbon Sauce)
½ cup water

Whisk until well mixed. Pour over meatloaf before serving.

Restaurant Recipe

Giovanni's

728 Boone Avenue
Winchester, KY 40391
859-745-2991

"The Italian Place to Be." This statement is proclaimed in neon at the front of Giovanni's Restaurant. When you visit, you will find a big menu of Italian favorites and a buffet featuring plenty of delicious food to satisfy all your Italian cravings. A local favorite is the baked spaghetti, and you'll also find naked noodles with Bolognese, marinara, and Alfredo sauces so you can fix the pasta to suit your

fancy. All are delicious. Pizza options include pepperoni, cheese, ham, sausage, banana peppers, mushrooms, and more. The salad bar is the freshest in town and you won't want to miss Giovanni's Special Red Dressing. All of this, at an affordable price and topped off by a friendly and always attentive wait staff, truly makes Giovanni's the Italian place to be.

Monday – Saturday:
11:00 am to 10:00 pm

Mint Julep

1 ounce Mint Simple Syrup

2 ounces bourbon

Crushed ice or ice cubes

In a serving glass, combine minted simple syrup, bourbon and a splash of water. Add ice to almost fill glass; stir well. Garnish with a mint sprig, if desired.

Mint Simple Syrup:

1 cup water

1 cup sugar

1 bunch mint

In saucepan over medium heat, stir together water and sugar until sugar dissolves. Bring to a simmer and simmer 5 minutes, stirring occasionally. Remove from heat. Add mint and steep 15 minutes. Strain, then refrigerate syrup until cold, about 3 hours. (Can be prepared up to 1 week ahead. Cover and keep refrigerated.)

Local Favorite

THINKSTOCK/ ISTOCK/ BHOFACK2

Hot Cheese Squares

4 eggs

Salt and pepper

8 ounces shredded Cheddar cheese

8 ounces shredded Pepper Jack cheese

Season eggs with salt and pepper to taste and beat slightly. Stir in cheese. Pour into a treated 8x8-inch casserole dish. Bake at 375° for 30 minutes. Cut into squares to serve.

Note: This recipe can be easily doubled baked in a 9x13-inch dish and freezes well.

Local Favorite

Bourbon Ball Candy

1 (16-ounce) package powdered sugar

⅓ cup bourbon (the better the bourbon, the better the candy)

1 stick butter, softened

1½ cups pecan halves

1 (12-ounce) package semisweet chocolate morsels

1 tablespoon shortening

Stir sugar, bourbon and butter until well blended. Cover and refrigerate 8 hours. Shape into 1-inch balls. Press one pecan half into the top of each ball. Refrigerate another 8 hours. Melt chocolate and shortening in a saucepan over medium heat; remove from heat. Dip bourbon balls in chocolate, and place on wax paper. Refrigerate at least 1 hour before serving.

Local Favorite

Italian Balsamic Bruschetta

8 Roma (plum) tomatoes, diced

⅓ cup chopped fresh basil

¼ cup shredded Parmesan cheese

2 cloves garlic, minced

1 tablespoon balsamic vinegar

1 teaspoon olive oil

¼ teaspoon salt

¼ teaspoon black pepper

1 loaf French bread, sliced and toasted

Place tomatoes in a bowl. Add basil, Parmesan cheese and garlic; toss to mix well. Carefully mix in balsamic vinegar, olive oil, salt and pepper. Serve on toasted bread slices. Serves 8.

Local Favorite

THINKSTOCK/ ISTOCK/ BHOFACK2

Eastern REGION

Chimney Corner Café

1624 Carter Avenue
Ashland, KY 41101
606-324-7500

Located in the heart of downtown Ashland for more than seventy-five years, Chimney Corner Café is a unique restaurant offering casual fare in a friendly, cozy environment. Chef Paul Runnels has owned the business since 2001 and makes everything from scratch using only the freshest ingredients. Always fresh, never frozen, the food is the star at Chimney Corner where you will enjoy lobster bisque, French onion soup, and high quality beef. The seasonal menu is modified every few weeks and everything is always delicious. Classic Kentucky Hot Brown is a local favorite of sliced ham and turkey topped with soft bread then covered in Mornay sauce, tomatoes, and bacon. If you are looking for outstanding, freshly prepared dishes, a unique atmosphere, and exceptional service, Chimney Corner Café is the place to go.

Tuesday – Saturday: 4:00 pm to 9:00 pm

Pumpkin Pie Cheesecake Spread

2 (8-ounce) packages cream cheese, softened
¼ cup packed brown sugar
1 teaspoon pumpkin pie spice
½ teaspoon maple flavoring, optional
Vanilla wafers

Beat cream cheese until light and fluffy. Add brown sugar and spice; beat until mixed well. Add flavoring; stir until well blended. Serve with vanilla wafers.

Local Favorite

NATURAL BRIDGE
Slade

Natural Bridge, a natural sandstone arch, is sixty-five feet high and spans seventy-eight feet. Though there are a number of rock formations throughout the United States called natural bridges, this is one of only a few that you can actually walk across. You can also walk under it by way of "Fat Man's Squeeze," a narrow passage in the rock formation that leads to the bottom of the arch.

Natural Bridge State Park, home to Natural Bridge, has some of the most unique geological formations and breathtaking views found anywhere in the state. With 2,200 acres, twenty-two miles of trails, and a sixty-acre lake, there are plenty of activities to enjoy—hiking, camping, and wildlife viewing. For those not up to the adventure of hiking to Natural Bridge, a Skylift is available that takes you close. And if one day is not enough, you may opt to stay at one of the two campgrounds or local lodge.

After viewing the Natural Bridge, don't miss Balanced Rock—a single piece of sandstone weathered in such a fashion that its midsection is narrower than its cap or its base. It is one of the biggest and best examples east of the Rocky Mountains.

Natural Bridge State Resort Park
2135 Natural Bridge Road • Slade, KY 40376
606-663-2214 • www.parks.ky.gov

JJ Family Restaurant

5260 13th Street
Ashland, KY 41102
606-325-3816
www.jjfamilyrestaurant.com

JJ's Southern hospitality and good ol' country cooking are the next best thing to grandma's house. Whether you prefer pinto beans and cornbread, boneless chicken breast fried in grandma's iron skillet, or a tender rib-eye steak grilled on an open flame, they serve the best—just for you. Don't forget to save some room for made-from-scratch desserts that are sure to leave you with a smile. If you are looking for a Christian atmosphere with friends, smiles, big portions, and bigger flavor, then look no further than JJ's.

Monday – Saturday: 6:00 am to 9:00 pm
Sunday: 11:00 am to 6:00 pm

JJ's Potato Soup

4 sticks butter
2 gallons diced potatoes
½ pound American cheese
½ gallon (2 quarts) whipping cream
Salt to taste
Pepper to taste
½ cup chopped chives

Melt butter in bottom of large stockpot; add diced potatoes. Add water to cover. Cook, stirring often, over medium heat for approximately 1 hour or until tender. Add cheese and cream and heat until cheese has melted. Add salt and pepper to taste. Stir in chives.

Restaurant Recipe

JJ's Cornbread

2 cups oil (preferably vegetable oil)
5 cups self-rising flour
5 cups cornmeal
1 quart buttermilk
Water if needed

Preheat oven to 450°. Once oven is hot, pour oil into a 12x17-inch pan and insert into oven. Mix flour and cornmeal in a bowl. Add buttermilk and mix with a spoon about 5 minutes or until lumps are dissolved. The consistency should be similar to waffle batter (slightly thicker than pancake batter). If batter is too thick, add small amounts of water until it is the right consistency.

By now, oil should be hot. (Note that the hotter you get the oil, the better the cornbread will turn out.) Carefully remove pan from oven and pour three quarters of the oil into batter. Quickly and carefully fold oil into batter. Pour batter into hot pan. You may notice oil pooling in corners of pan. If this happens, use your spoon to draw some of the oil out and put it in center of batter.

Place pan on center rack in oven. Cook 15 minutes, then turn pan and cook another 10 minutes or until top is golden brown. Remove from oven and flip cornbread onto a cooling rack. Cool 10 minutes before cutting.

Restaurant Recipe

JJ's Peanut Butter Fudge Cake

1½ cups flour
1 cup sugar
1 cup brown sugar
3 eggs, beaten
3 sticks butter, softened (divided)
1¾ cups peanut butter (divided)
1 (7-ounce) jar marshmallow cream
½ cup milk
1 (16-ounce) box powdered sugar plus more if needed

Mix flour, sugar, brown sugar, eggs, 2 sticks butter and 1 cup peanut butter in a bowl. Pour into a greased 9x13-inch baking pan. Bake at 325° for 30 minutes. Immediately spread marshmallow cream on hot cake.

Bring remaining stick butter and milk to boil; remove from heat. Add remaining ¾ cup peanut butter and powdered sugar. More powdered sugar may be added to reach the correct consistency. Pour fudge over cake; cool before cutting.

Restaurant Recipe

V.I.P.'s Place

1480 Highway 90
Bronston, KY 42518
606-561-3749

There is good reason for the popularity of V.I.P.'s Place, because the food has real "pulling power" and draws people from many miles around. It is as close to home cooking as you can get. At V.I.P.'s Place you will find friendly surroundings and each and every order receives prompt attention. Everything served is prepared from top-quality ingredients by cooks who know how to please your taste buds. Enjoy a full breakfast or biscuits with a variety of meats, then come back for a plate lunch Monday through Friday, or order off the menu to enjoy hamburgers, country fried steaks, fish, shrimp, wings, and more. Family-owned and operated since 1998, the owners at V.I.P.'s Place are proud of their establishment and for good reason—when you visit, you will find the best in food, service, and prices. Breakfast and lunch, they are sure to satisfy in every respect.

Monday – Saturday: 5:30 am to 3:00 pm

Apple Dumplin's

4 Granny Smith apples
2 (8-ounce) cans crescent rolls
2 sticks butter
1½ cups sugar
1 teaspoon cinnamon
1 (16-ounce) bottle ginger ale

Peel, core and quarter apples. Separate crescent dough into triangles. Roll each apple piece in 1 triangle and place in a greased 9x13-inch baking dish. In a saucepan over medium-low heat, melt butter; stir in sugar and cinnamon and blend together until sugar is dissolved. Pour over dumplings. Pour ginger ale around edge of dumplings (but not enough to cover top of dumplings). Bake at 350° for 30 to 45 minutes. Serve warm with a scoop of vanilla ice cream. Makes 16 dumplings.

Restaurant Recipe

Brussels Sprout Chiffonade

1 pound Brussels sprouts
1 (12-ounce) package uncured bacon
½ medium yellow onion
1 large shallot
¼ teaspoon fresh cracked pepper
Agave syrup, optional

Cut ends off Brussels sprouts and remove loose outer layers. Cut each Brussels sprout in half then slice each as thinly as possible (chiffonade). Dice and separate bacon into pan over medium heat. Dice onion and shallot; add to bacon along with pepper. Cook until 80% of desired doneness is achieved. Drain bacon and onions (leave as much fat as desired). Add Brussels sprouts and raise heat to medium-high. Cook, while stirring or tossing the mixture, until Brussels sprouts are bright green. Continue to cook, while tossing, for about 30 seconds to 1 minute. Bright green will be the least bitter and will have nutty sweetness, so don't overcook. For extra sweetness, a drizzle of agave is perfect. Serve hot.

Restaurant Recipe

Red River Rockhouse

4000 Route 11
Campton, KY 41301
606-668-6656
www.redriverrockhouse.com

Red River Rockhouse is a family-owned, farm-to-table restaurant featuring American classics and Mexican favorites using all locally-sourced beef, pork, chicken, and eggs. All the produce is hand selected for the best freshness and local produce is used whenever available. Weekend specials are made in-house by the owner. Local favorites include Red River Rockhouse's homemade carrot cake and coffee. Also available is craft beer on tap, including local brews, and many bottled favorites.

Open March through December
Thursday, Friday & Monday:
Noon to 9:00 pm
Saturday & Sunday: 8:30 am to 9:00 pm

Kathy's Country Kitchen

20 Black Creek Road
Clay City, KY 40312
606-663-4179

A visit to Kathy's Country Kitchen is like stepping back in time to grandmother's table to enjoy good, country comfort food. Kathy uses many of her own grandmother's recipes like the delicious Waldorf Salad. With Kathy's grandmother's dishes on display and wooden tables and chairs from another era, the restaurant has the feel of yesterday. Even the restroom is like stepping into an outhouse. From fresh vegetables to the sweetest onion rings ever, from pies with mile-high meringue to catfish and coleslaw, to steaks and ribs cooked on a grill outside, Kathy's old-fashioned cooking never disappoints.

Monday – Thursday: 6:00 am to 10:00 pm
Friday & Saturday: 6:00 am to 10:30 pm
Sunday: 11:00 am to 2:00 pm

Pork Chops with Chipotle Cranberry Glaze

¼ teaspoon salt

¼ teaspoon sugar

¼ teaspoon ground cinnamon

4 boneless pork loin chops

1 tablespoon olive oil

1 cup fresh cranberries

¼ cup orange juice

2 tablespoons dried cranberries

2 tablespoons red wine vinegar

1 tablespoon chopped chipotle pepper in adobo sauce

1 tablespoon orange marmalade

1 garlic clove, minced

2 tablespoons sliced almonds, toasted

1 tablespoon thinly sliced green onion

In a small bowl, combine salt, sugar and cinnamon. Sprinkle over pork chops. In a large skillet, cook chops (uncovered) in oil over medium heat for 6 to 8 minutes on each side, or until meat juices run clear. Remove to a serving platter and keep warm. In the same skillet, combine cranberries, orange juice, dried cranberries, vinegar, chipotle pepper, marmalade and garlic. Cook and stir 2 to 3 minutes or until heated through. Spoon over chops; sprinkle with almonds and green onions.

Restaurant Recipe

NOLONELY/ISTOCK/THINKSTOCK

Waldorf Salad

1 cup mayonnaise
½ cup sugar
3 Gala apples, diced
¾ cup chopped walnuts
2 celery stalks, finely chopped
½ cup raisins
½ cup marshmallows

Combine mayonnaise and sugar; blend well. Combine remaining ingredients and stir in mayonnaise mixture; mix well. Chill and serve.

Restaurant Recipe

Strawberry Pretzel Salad

1 (12-ounce) bag pretzels
½ stick butter, melted
1 pound fresh strawberries
1 (16-ounce) bag strawberry glaze
1 (8-ounce) package cream cheese, softened
1 (8-ounce) carton whipped topping
½ cup sugar

Finely crush pretzels and add enough butter to hold pretzel crumbs together; press into baking sheet. Bake at 350° for 8 minutes; cool. Wash and slice strawberries, add glaze and set aside. Blend cream cheese, whipped topping and sugar until smooth. Spread creamed mixture over cooled crust. Top with strawberry mixture and chill before serving.

Restaurant Recipe

MYCHKOALEZANDER/ISTOCK/THINKSTOCK

Colonel Harland Sanders Museum & Café

I-75, Exit 29
US Highway 25 E & 25 W
Corbin, KY 40701
606-528-2163

Eat Where It All Began[SM]

Experience just what it was like in 1940 to dine at the Colonel Harland Sanders Café in Corbin, Kentucky. Colonel Sanders' original restaurant, where Kentucky Fried Chicken® got its start, has been carefully restored and reopened to the public. Enjoy a delicious meal at the Café (which is on the National Register of Historic Places), and view Colonel Harland Sanders exhibits. Admission is free to the fascinating artifacts and memorabilia from the early days of the KFC® restaurant system. Still serving the Colonel's Original Recipe® Chicken with its secret herbs and spices!

Monday – Sunday: 10:00 am to 10:00 pm
(winter hours 9:00 pm)

Southern Spoon Bread

You don't have to be a Southerner to enjoy this casserole dish.

3 cups milk
1 teaspoon salt
1 teaspoon sugar
1¼ cups cornmeal
3 eggs
3 teaspoons baking powder
2 tablespoons cold water
2 tablespoons butter, softened

In a saucepan over medium heat, warm milk, salt and sugar to a moderate temperature. Add cornmeal and mix well. Cook to a mush then remove from heat to cool slightly. In a separate bowl, beat together eggs, baking powder, water and butter. Beat egg mixture into mush. Pour into 8-inch square casserole dish or pan. Bake at 400° about 25 to 30 minutes.

Eula Gibson, Food Supervisor,
Sanders Restaurant
Family Favorite

Crabmeat Salad

2½ pounds shredded crabmeat,
cooked and cooled

½ stalk celery, diced

5 green onions, diced

Juice of 2 lemons

¼ tablespoon dry mustard

3 ounces (6 tablespoons) mayonnaise

Mix together; chill 2 hours. Serves 10.

Restaurant Recipe

Cornbread Salad

12 cornbread muffins (cold), shredded

2 small red onions, diced

2 green bell peppers, diced

1 cup shredded Cheddar cheese

2 medium tomatoes, diced

12 bread and butter pickle slices, diced

8 cooked and cooled sausage patties,
diced

3 ounces (6 tablespoons) mayonnaise,
or more to taste

Mix all ingredients together except mayonnaise; add mayonnaise using a little more, if necessary, to reach desired consistency. Chill 2 hours. Serves 20 people.

Restaurant Recipe

David's Steakhouse & Buffet

**125 West Cumberland Gap Parkway
Corbin, KY 40701
606-528-0063**

Located on Interstate 75 at exit 29 on the beautiful Cumberland Gap Parkway, David's Steakhouse has been butchering choice steaks and providing a home-cooked buffet since 1985. You will enjoy their great selection of homemade soups, cold salads, and southern comfort food. Experience a friendly, down-home atmosphere that will not break your wallet! If you're planning a family reunion, banquet, company picnic, or wedding, David's Steakhouse will meet your catering needs with a customized plan for your event. Stop and visit on your next trip to Corbin.

**Sunday – Thursday: 11:00 am to 9:00 pm
Friday & Saturday: 11:00 am to 10:00 pm**

Depot on Main

101 North Main Street
Corbin, KY 40701
606-523-1117
www.depotonmain.com

The Depot on Main is a premier steakhouse offering a luxurious dining experience in a friendly, comfortable, and sophisticated environment. Only the best Certified Angus Beef is served after grilling on a custom, high-temperature ceramic grill searing in the juices and seasonings ensuring each succulent steak is perfectly prepared. Select from fresh seafood, our mouthwatering pastas, garden fresh salads, and sandwiches. Sit back, relax, and let the friendly staff ensure you have a wonderful dining experience. For some local flavor, the spacious full-service bar is a favorite place to relax, hang out, and enjoy a cocktail or an ice cold beer. While enjoying your favorite spirits, be sure to treat yourself to one of many delicious signature appetizers, such as Blue Cheese Chips, Sausage Stuffed Mushrooms, Fried Banana Peppers or Rick's Famous Beer Cheese. Owned and operated by Holly Curry, the Depot on Main is ready to serve you . . . deliciously.

Monday – Saturday: 4:00 pm to Closing

Italian Cream Cake

½ cup margarine, softened
½ cup vegetable shortening
2 cups sugar
5 eggs, separated
2 cups all-purpose flour
1 teaspoon baking soda
1 cup buttermilk
1 teaspoon vanilla
1 (4-ounce) can flaked coconut
1 cup chopped walnuts

Cream margarine and shortening. Add sugar gradually, beating until smooth. Add egg yolks, beat well. Combine flour and baking soda; add to creamed mixture alternating with buttermilk. Stir in vanilla, coconut and nuts. Beat egg whites until stiff; fold into batter. Pour into 3 greased 8-inch cake pans. Bake in preheated 350° oven for 25 minutes. Cool.

Cream Cheese Frosting:

1 (8-ounce) block cream cheese, softened
¼ cup margarine
1 (16-ounce) box powdered sugar
1 teaspoon vanilla
Chopped nuts, optional

Beat all frosting ingredients, except nuts, together until smooth. Spread between layers and top and sides of cake. Sprinkle top with chopped nuts, if desired.

Restaurant Recipe

Hot Dog Chili

3 pounds hamburger meat

1 cup water

3 teaspoons salt

5 tablespoons Mexican chili powder

1 (15-ounce) can tomato sauce

1 tablespoon Franks Red Hot Sauce

1 cup crushed cornflakes

Cook hamburger, water and salt for 20 minutes in saucepan over medium-high heat. Drain off some grease. Add chili powder, tomato sauce, hot sauce and cornflake crumbs. Cook another 20 minutes, adding more water if too thick.

Restaurant Recipe

Peanut Butter Fudge

1½ sticks butter,
plus more for treating pan

3 cups sugar

⅔ cup (5 ounces) evaporated milk

¾ cup peanut butter

1 (7-ounce) jar marshmallow cream

Butter a 9x13-inch pan. In saucepan over medium heat, melt butter; stir in sugar and evaporated milk. Stirring constantly, bring to a boil. Boil 5 minutes. Remove from heat, and quickly stir in peanut butter and marshmallow cream until fully incorporated. Pour into buttered pan. Let set until firm. Cut and serve.

Restaurant Recipe

J & B Country Cooking

**2014 South Main Street
Corbin, KY 40701
606-528-9555
www.facebook.com/
JandBCountryCooking**

J & B Country Cooking is a family-owned and operated restaurant located in Corbin, Kentucky. J & B offers daily lunch and dinner specials as well as a menu that offers a variety of burgers, sandwiches, salads, and other dinners as well as desserts made fresh daily.

**Monday – Friday: 7:00 am to 7:00 pm
Saturday: 6:30 am to 3:00 pm**

Smokey Bear's BBQ

Smokey Bear's Barbecue, LLC

1509 American Greeting Card Road
Corbin, KY 40701
606-523-2233
www.smokeybearsbarbecue.com

Smokey Bear's Barbecue is the product of former Kentucky police officer Barry Mays and his wife Leanne when they took a leap of faith and decided they wanted to sell pig for a living. Smokey Bear's offers delicious smoked pulled pork, baby back ribs, fresh hand-crafted burgers, beef brisket, hand-breaded made-to-order catfish, fried bologna, barbecue and Buffalo wings, and much, much more. The outstanding barbecue is slow smoked with hickory wood, and the barbecue sauces are all made from scratch and taste like nothing you have ever tried. Be sure to include an order of Smokey Bear's homemade fresh-cut fries with your meal. Don't miss Smokey Bear's Barbecue where the 'que is sure to please.

Monday – Friday: 10:30 am to 8:00 pm
Saturday: 11:00 am to 5:00 pm

Smokey Bear's Homemade Southern-Style Coleslaw

2½ pounds cabbage, shredded or diced
4 to 5 ounces shredded or diced carrots
2 cups mayonnaise
¾ tablespoon distilled vinegar
1½ cups sugar
½ tablespoon celery seed
½ tablespoon celery salt

Shred or dice cabbage and carrots to the texture of your liking into a large serving bowl. In a separate bowl, whisk mayonnaise, vinegar and sugar until mixed well. Add celery seed and celery salt; whisk well. Pour over cabbage mixture and mix well. Cover and refrigerate about 2 hours or until ready to serve. Makes a delicious southern sweet slaw to eat on the side or put on a barbecue sandwich.

Restaurant Recipe

MOONBOW AT CUMBERLAND FALLS
Corbin

Rainbows aren't the only "bows" in the sky. When moonlight refracts in waterdrops and causes a pale colored bow, the results are moonbows. An example of this phenomenon is the mist emitted from Kentucky's biggest waterfall, Cumberland Falls, during a full moon on a clear night. For longer than time has recorded, people have been drawn to this wondrous sight, and to this day the rare natural phenomenon draws hundreds of visitors each year to Cumberland Falls State Resort Park.

Although moonbows can occur periodically at other waterfalls, only two in the world can be seen on a predicted schedule—Cumberland Falls near Corbin, Kentucky, USA and Victoria Falls, Zimbabwe, Africa. The moonbow in Kentucky usually occurs two days before and two days after the full moon. An arch of white light is usually produced at the base of the Falls and continues downstream. The arch contains the colors of the spectrum in consecutive bands (which can be seen in photographs taken with long exposure), but appears white to the naked eye due to the low amount of sunlight reflecting off of the moon.

www.parks.ky.gov

Cornbread Café

1141 Highway 36 • Frenchburg, KY 40322
606-768-3125

The Cornbread Café offers a casual and family-friendly atmosphere. By serving both home-cooked meals as well as many fast-food options, Cornbread Café's menu is sure to please everyone. Dine-in, call-in or drive thru, however you choose to order it, their food tastes great every time. Fill up at the daily buffet which offers delicious home-cooked dishes. You won't leave hungry at the Cornbread Café!

Monday – Thursday: 5:00 am to 9:00 pm
Friday: 5:00 am to 10:00 pm
Saturday: 7:00 am to 10:00 pm
Sunday: 8:00 am to 9:00 pm

Cornbread

5 cups self-rising cornmeal

2 tablespoons sugar

3 eggs, beaten

3 cups buttermilk

1 cup whole milk

½ cup melted lard

4 tablespoons lard, for pans

Preheat oven to 375°. Combine dry ingredients. Add eggs, buttermilk, milk and ½ cup melted lard. Mix well, but DO NOT over-stir. Place 2 tablespoons lard in each of 2 (9x13-inch) pans and put in oven to get hot (only a minute or 2; just until lard is melted). Pour cornbread mixture evenly into pans. Bake 20 to 25 minutes, or until golden brown. Serve warm with fresh sweet cream butter. Serves 24.

Restaurant Recipe

Old-Fashioned Soup Beans

1 pound dry pinto beans

¼ pound smoked jowl bacon

1 teaspoon salt

3 tablespoons lard

Wash beans and pick through to make sure they are cleaned thoroughly and all rocks are removed. Fill a 4-quart stockpot about two thirds full with water. Remove skin from smoked jowl bacon and discard skin. Cut jowl bacon into chunks and add to stockpot, along with beans. Add salt and lard. Cook over medium heat 3 hours, adding water as needed.

Restaurant Recipe

Stuffed Mushrooms

½ cup shredded Swiss cheese

1 hard-boiled egg, finely chopped

3 tablespoons finely crushed breadcrumbs

1 teaspoon minced garlic

2 tablespoons butter, softened

1 pound fresh mushrooms

4 tablespoons melted butter

In a bowl, combine cheese, egg, breadcrumbs, garlic and 2 tablespoons softened butter. Preheat oven to broil. Remove stems from mushrooms and place each, round side up, on a baking sheet. Brush tops with melted butter. Broil about 4 inches from heat for 2 to 3 minutes or just until lightly brown. Remove from broiler and flip mushrooms. Fill with cheese mixture. Broil another 2 minutes. Makes about 36 stuffed mushrooms.

Local Favorite

New Potatoes in Caper Sauce

12 small new potatoes, scrubbed clean

1 stick butter

Salt and pepper to taste

1 teaspoon vinegar

2 tablespoons minced capers

2 tablespoons minced fresh parsley

½ cup grated Parmesan cheese

1 tablespoon minced green onion

Boil potatoes (skin on) in salted water to cover until tender. Combine remaining ingredients in a saucepan over medium heat. When potatoes are tender, drain and add to sauce. Cook until heated through. When serving, spoon sauce over potatoes.

Local Favorite

THINKSTOCK/ ISTOCK/ ROSEMARY BUFFONI

Pecan Pumpkin Muffins

2½ cups all-purpose flour

½ cup sugar

¼ cup packed brown sugar

2 teaspoons pumpkin pie spice

1 teaspoon baking powder

1 teaspoon baking soda

½ teaspoon salt

2 eggs

1 cup canned pumpkin purée

½ cup buttermilk

¼ cup canola oil

1 teaspoon vanilla extract

½ cup chopped pecans

Combine dry ingredients in a large bowl. In another bowl, combine eggs, pumpkin, buttermilk, oil and vanilla. Stir into dry ingredients just until moistened. Fold in pecans. Fill 12 greased or paper-lined muffin cups three-fourths full.

Topping:

⅓ cup packed brown sugar

⅓ cup finely chopped pecans

¼ cup all-purpose flour

1 stick cold butter, cubed

In a small bowl, combine topping ingredients, cutting in butter until crumbly. Sprinkle over batter. Bake at 375° for 25 to 30 minutes or until a toothpick inserted near the center comes out clean. Cool for 5 minutes before removing from pan to a wire rack. Serve warm. Yields 12 muffins.

Local Favorite

Johnny's Pizza

117 West Main
Grayson, KY 41143
606-474-2441

A hometown favorite since 1953, Johnny's Pizza follows an age-old tradition of making pizza using timeless recipes that have been passed down through generations. With smell of spices and homemade dishes filling the air, you will want to make it your home away from home. Tempt your taste buds with Johnny's lasagna or spaghetti dinners. Or perhaps you would prefer a chicken, steak or meatball sub. And, of course, the pizza is the best. A local favorite is the Hawaiian pizza. Johnny's

 also offers delicious daily specials. As they say, "Taste the difference in our fresh made pizza!"

Tuesday – Thursday: 11:00 am to 9:00 pm
Friday & Saturday: 11:00 am to 10:00 pm
Sunday: 11:00 am to 9:00 pm

Cookie Monster Salad

A favorite with the children and so easy they can make it themselves.

2 (3.4-ounce) packages vanilla instant pudding
1½ cups half-and-half
1 (12-ounce) carton whipped topping
1 (12-ounce) package fudge striped cookies
1 (20-ounce) can blueberry pie filling

Beat pudding and half-and-half until thick; fold in whipped topping. Break half the cookies in small pieces and add to pudding mixture. Spread half of this mixture into the bottom of a large, glass bowl or trifle dish. Top with blueberry pie filling then remaining pudding mixture. Break remaining cookies in half and place cut-side down along sides of dish. Refrigerate before serving. Serves 10 to 12 cookie monsters.

Note: Strawberry pie filling or 1 (11-ounce) can mandarin oranges (drained) and 1 (8-ounce) can pineapple tidbits (drained) can be substituted for the blueberry pie filling with equally delicious results.

Local Favorite

Chicken and Dumplings

5 pounds chicken breasts

½ cup chicken base

Place chicken and chicken base in a large pot with water to cover. Cook over medium heat until done, about 2 hours. Remove chicken; cool then shred. Increase heat under broth to high to bring to rolling boil.

2½ to 3 pounds self-rising flour

1 cup milk

2 tablespoons vegetable oil

Cold water, approximately 2 cups

Mix flour, milk and oil together; add cold water until thick enough to drop by spoonfuls into boiling broth. In the midst of dropping dumplings, reduce heat to low. Cook about 5 minutes after last dumpling is dropped. Remove from heat and let set 5 minutes. Add shredded chicken. Serve.

Restaurant Recipe

Country Kitchen

Biscuits & Gravy

7200 Kentucky 979
Grethel, KY 41631
606-587-2550

Serving the delicious dishes you remember eating as a kid, Country Kitchen has been a staple in Grethel for twelve years. From hot soups, fresh salads, and hand-pattied burgers, to homemade desserts like German Upside Down Cake, Better than Anything Cake, and Hot Fudge Cake and pies such as Banana Cream Pie and Coconut Cream Pie, Country Kitchen serves the food you love. Daily specials are available every Monday to Friday. Come in and visit Ms. Christine and her girls and taste the foods that bring back the memories of childhood. Catering is also available.

Monday – Saturday: 7:00 am to 8:00 pm

The Twin

63 River Drive
Irvine, KY 40336
606-723-5623

Established in 1959 and still owned and operated by the original family, The Twin got its name because there were five sets of twins within about a three block area around the restaurant. The Twin is a walk-up restaurant serving the same items—nothing fried—since they started in 1959. You'll love the hot dogs, Coney's (hot dog with chili), chili bun, hot ham and cheese with special sauce, BBQ sandwiches, chips, coke, Ale-8-One, and the highest quality ice cream served in cones, as a sundae or Twizzards, and as dip top cones in cherry, chocolate or butterscotch. The Twin, a mainstay in the small town of Irvine, is the place where you can see everyone, meet friends after school or on game days, and where everyone goes for ice cream after they win the big game—and even if they lose.

Sunday – Thursday:
10:30 am to 10:00 pm

Friday & Saturday:
10:30 am to 11:00 pm

Hot Fudge Cake

Served at The Twin since its opening in 1959

2½ cups flour

1½ teaspoons baking soda

½ teaspoon salt

2 cups sugar

1½ sticks butter, melted

3 eggs

2 teaspoons vanilla

1 cup buttermilk

¾ cup cocoa

½ cup water

Sift together flour, baking soda and salt. Add remaining ingredients; mix well. Line the bottoms of 2 (9x11-inch) pans with wax paper. Divide batter evenly between pans. Bake 25 minutes at 350°.

Restaurant Recipe

Avenue Café

1915 Cumberland Avenue
Middlesboro, KY 40965
606-248-5179

If you're looking for a down-home meal, daily specials, burgers, all-day breakfast, and delicious desserts, visit the Avenue Café. Experience the rich history of Middlesboro on the walls of the café where every mayor of the Magic City—the city created from a crater—is pictured. While there, you will enjoy delicious food, great service, and a terrific atmosphere. On Fridays and Saturdays Avenue Café serves mouth-watering ribs, smoked on a grill and covered with their signature barbeque sauce, plus rib-eyes and sirloin steaks from the grill, and more. So if you're in the mood for a special dining experience, stop by and visit. You'll be glad you did.

WINTER HOURS:
Monday – Thursday: 7:00 am to 6:30 pm
Friday & Saturday: 7:00 am to 9:00 pm

SUMMER HOURS:
Monday – Thursday 7:00 am to 7:00 pm
Friday & Saturday 7:00 am to 9:00 pm

Avenue Café's Kentucky Country Meatloaf

10 pounds ground chuck

1 large onion, diced

1 large green pepper, diced

2 sleeves saltine crackers

¼ cup Worcestershire sauce

1 cup ketchup

3 eggs, beaten

Salt, pepper and other seasoning to taste

Ketchup for topping

Combine all ingredients, except ketchup, mixing well. Shape into 1 large loaf in a 12x17-inch pan. Bake at 350° for 45 minutes. Cover with ketchup, slice and serve. We serve it with mashed potatoes, green beans and a roll.

Restaurant Recipe

Shades Café & Steakhouse

2119 Cumberland Avenue
Middlesboro, KY 40965
606-248-4315

Shades Café & Steakhouse started as a rural independent coffee shop serving hot drinks and sandwiches in the afternoons and evenings. Since 2008, Shades has grown into a full café offering a variety of food from gourmet salads to savory piattos—an Italian flatbread pizza. On Friday and Saturday nights, the Café quickly turns into a full-service steakhouse serving the best C.A.B. steaks, shrimp, and chops in Eastern Kentucky. If you want to warm up with a bowl of soup, grab an espresso to go, or have a romantic evening meal in downtown Middlesboro, Shades has you covered.

Monday & Tuesday: 3:00 pm to 9:00 pm
Wednesday & Thursday:
11:00 am to 9:00 pm
Friday & Saturday: 3:00 pm to 10:00 pm

Chicken Bacon Ranch Piatto

Ranch dressing
1 piece herbed flat bread
¾ cup shredded mozzarella cheese, divided
¼ pound sliced grilled chicken
½ cup crumbled cooked bacon

Spread ranch dressing on 1 side of flat bread, top with ½ cup cheese, chicken and bacon. Grill approximately 10 minutes, or until cheese is melted. You can use a Panini grill, flat grill or stove top. Remove from grill and sprinkle with remaining mozzarella and drizzle ranch dressing on top.

Serve with chips and avocado dip.

Restaurant Recipe

Avocado Dip

5 avocados, halved, seeded and peeled
1 cup mayonnaise
¾ cup sour cream
¼ cup chopped onion
⅛ teaspoon garlic salt
Dash cayenne pepper
2 teaspoons Worcestershire sauce

Blend in food processor until smooth.

Restaurant Recipe

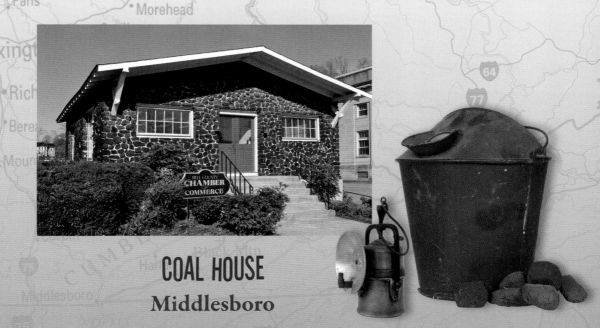

COAL HOUSE
Middlesboro

A truly unique landmark, the Coal House was built in 1926 using forty-two tons of bituminous coal and is now home to the Bell County Chamber of Commerce. When you visit, check out the Bell County Coal Mining Museum next door. It is an outdoor museum that features coal mining equipment from the 1960's.

Interestingly, the city was incorporated in 1890 as "Middlesborough," named after the town of Middlesbrough in England. The U.S. Post Office began using the spelling "Middlesboro" in 1894. Today, both spellings are used interchangeably.

Middlesboro also has the rare distinction of being the only city in the United States built entirely inside a crater. It is located between Pine Mountain and the Cumberland Mountains in the Middlesboro Basin, which geologists believe to be an enormous meteor crater—one of three known astroblemes in the state. What is an astrobleme? It is a mark on the earth's surface, usually circular, formed by a large ancient meteorite impact.

189 North 20th Street
Middlesboro, KY 40965
www.middlesborokentucky.net

COMMONWEALTH OF KENTUCKY

MIDDLESBORO METEORITE
CRATER IMPACT SITE
• • •
Designated by the Kentucky Society of Professional Geologists as a Distinguished Geological Site. Middlesboro is one of only a few cities on the North American continent located in the basin of a meteorite impact structure.   Over.

Presented by the Bell Co. Historical Society.

Family Diner

576 Highway 3106
Monticello, KY 42633
606-340-0816

Welcome to Family Diner—one of the best places to eat and work in Kentucky. From breakfast all day to fried potatoes, people have been known to drive up to 200 miles just to eat at Family Diner. Just ask the locals and they will tell you about "Catfish Fridays" where you eat the best fried catfish ever along with sides made fresh. Don't forget the desserts—chocolate cream pie and mouth-watering coconut cream pie are both made from scratch. Eating at Family Diner is just like eating at granny's table.

Monday – Saturday: 7:00 am to 8:00 pm
Sunday: 7:00 am to 3:00 pm

Family Diner Meatloaf

2 pounds ground beef
1 medium yellow onion, chopped
Salt and pepper to taste
1 cup rolled oats
4 to 5 eggs, beaten
1 cup ketchup plus more for topping

Preheat oven to 350°. Mix all ingredients together and form into a loaf. Cover top with additional ketchup to make a nice covering. Bake 1 to 1½ hours until done. Let set a few minutes before serving.

Restaurant Recipe

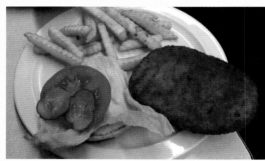

Sausage and Cheddar Scones

2 cups all-purpose flour

2 teaspoons baking powder

½ teaspoon baking soda

½ teaspoon salt

½ cup cold butter

¾ cup plus 2 tablespoons sour cream

1 egg, separated

12 ounces precooked sausage,
cubed or crumbled

2 cups shredded Cheddar cheese

2 tablespoons milk

Place first 4 ingredients in stand-up mixer bowl and mix well. Cut butter into small chunks and add to dry ingredients. With a flat beater, cut butter into dry ingredients until small crumbles form. Add sour cream and egg yolk, mix well until a stiff, sticky dough forms (a minute or so). Then add sausage and cheese and mix until well blended (30 seconds to 1 minute). Spoon individual scones on a baking sheet. (We use a 2-ounce scoop). You can also roll out as you would for biscuits and cut into approximately 12 to 14 pieces. Combine egg white with 2 tablespoons milk and brush tops of unbaked scones. Bake at 375° for 15 to 20 minutes. Remove from oven and serve warm. (Can be reheated in the microwave.)

Restaurant Recipe

Root-A-Bakers Bakery & Café

313 Flemingsburg Road
Morehead, KY 40351
606-780-4282
www.root-a-bakers.com

Root-A-Baker's is nestled within the heart of Morehead, Kentucky. Lana Root and her eight bakers spend their days baking for hungry customers. The smells of fresh baked breads and cookies in the bakery are overwhelming. Each first-time customer will receive a free sugar cookie as a way of saying "welcome to Root-A-Bakers." Not only does Root-A-Bakers cater to your sweet tooth, they also offer lunches featuring homemade chicken salad and pimento cheese on our fresh baked breads and warm creamy soups. Whether you drop by to satisfy a sweet tooth or to enjoy a complete meal, Root-A-Baker's is Morehead's best kept secret.

Tuesday – Friday: 7:00 am to 5:00 pm
Saturday: 8:00 am to 2:00 pm
Lunch reservations are encouraged.

Renfro Valley Lodge Restaurant

2380 Richmond Street
Mt. Vernon, KY 40456
800-765-7464
www.renfrovalley.com/the-lodge/

The historic Lodge Restaurant has been serving good ole' Kentucky country cooking and southern specialties since 1939 to the visitors of Renfro Valley Entertainment Center in Renfro Valley, Kentucky. Stop in between shows to taste the local flavor; the delicious hometown cooking is sure to please any appetite. The historic Lodge Restaurant is located just off I-75 at exit 62. While you're here, be sure to see one of our local Renfro Valley shows featuring classic country and bluegrass music in the Old Barn Theater or see a famous headliner in concert in the New Barn! For a full schedule, please visit our website!

Wednesday & Thursday:
11:00 am to 7:00 pm
Friday & Saturday: 7:00 am to 9:00 pm
Sunday: 7:00 am to 4:00 pm

Renfro Valley Lodge Restaurant Bread Pudding

Old bread or sandwich bread cut into 1-inch cubes
3 quarts milk
4 eggs, beaten
1 cup raisins
1 tablespoon vanilla extract
2 cups sugar
1 tablespoon salt
1 tablespoon cinnamon
½ tablespoon nutmeg

Fill a gallon container with bread, mashing the bread down in the container to be sure it is full. After measuring bread, place it in a 9x13-inch pan and spread it out evenly. Scald milk with all remaining ingredients and pour milk mixture over bread. Place in a preheated 350° oven and bake 25 minutes. Remove and cool to room temperature. Store in refrigerator. ENJOY!

Restaurant Recipe

Harbor Restaurant's Signature Salsa

½ cup finely chopped green onions, roots removed

½ cup finely chopped green bell pepper

¼ cup finely chopped jalapeño pepper

¼ bunch fresh cilantro, chopped

1 (64-ounce) can diced tomatoes

Sea salt and pepper

Combine green onions, bell pepper, jalapeño pepper and cilantro in a food processor with just a little juice from the canned tomatoes. Blend until all ingredients are finely ground. In a large bowl, combine canned tomatoes and blended ingredients; season to taste with sea salt and pepper. Serve with warm tortilla chips. Makes 8 to 9 cups.

Restaurant Recipe

Harbor Restaurant

451 Lee's Ford Dock Road
Nancy, KY 42544
606-636-4587
www.leesfordmarina.com

Overlooking beautiful Lake Cumberland, Harbor Restaurant is open daily for lunch and dinner. Famous for grouper, portobello mushroom fries, southern-fried banana peppers, and house-made chips and salsa, the vast menu is bound to satisfy every palette. The Harbor also serves unique pastas, steaks, and chicken dishes. Whether you are coming in from a day on the lake or just looking for that special place, Harbor Restaurant will be a one of a kind dining experience.

Monday – Thursday: 11:00 am to 9:00 pm
Friday & Saturday: 11:00 am to Midnight
Sunday: 11:00 am to 8:00 pm

Bob's BBQ

918 Clubhouse Drive
Prestonsburg, KY 41653
606-205-2477 or 606-886-2376

Bob's BBQ, established January 2000 in Pikeville, moved in 2006 to Stonecrest Golf Course in Prestonsburg. The restaurant provides services to the golf course and events at this location and outside catering services. Bob's specialty is barbecue pork, ribs, and brisket as well as steak and chicken. His signature BBQ sauce is available for purchase. The beautiful setting nestled in the foothills of the Appalachian Mountains is a must see. Down-home country cooking as well as a variety of sandwiches are offered at the snack bar. Friendly people and delicious food is what Bob's is all about. Go and see them soon.

Daily: 9:00 am to 5:00 pm

Chocolate Walnut Pie

½ cup butter, softened
¾ cup sugar
½ cup all-purpose flour
2 eggs
1 tablespoon bourbon
¾ cup semisweet chocolate chips
1 cup chopped walnuts
1 (8-inch) pie crust

Preheat oven to 350°. In a mixing bowl, cream butter and sugar together. Mix in flour. Beat eggs slightly, add to creamed mixture and mix. Stir in bourbon. Spread chocolate chips and nuts in bottom of pie shell. Pour filling over top. Bake at 350° for 30 to 40 minutes.

Local Favorite

Lizzie B's
Island Macaroni Salad

This simple yet delicious macaroni salad recipe was inspired by the typical lunch fare in Hawaii, typically referred to as the "plate lunch," where a couple scoops of rice and macaroni salad accompany a meat/protein of some sort. Bring this macaroni salad to your next family get-together, barbecue, picnic, or keep it all to yourself.

8 cups elbow macaroni

2 cups apple cider vinegar

4 cups Hellmann's mayonnaise

1 cup brown sugar

1 tablespoon kosher salt

1 tablespoon black pepper

2 carrots, finely shredded

1 bunch scallions, finely chopped

Cook macaroni until done; drain (do not rinse) and add to large, shallow bowl. Add apple cider vinegar and stir until macaroni is evenly coated. Cover and store in refrigerator until macaroni is completely cool. In a large bowl, combine mayonnaise, brown sugar, salt and pepper. Stir well. Add cooled macaroni and mix by hand until macaroni is evenly coated. If it seems too thick, you can add a little milk to thin. Add carrots and scallions to the mixture and mix by hand. Chill or eat it at room temperature. It's delicious either way.

Restaurant Recipe

Lizzie B's Café Bakery

2010 KY Route 321
Prestonsburg, KY 41653
606-886-2844
www.facebook.com/LizzieBCafe

Lizzie B's is like no other place in the region and is described as unique, eclectic, and a place you must visit in Eastern Kentucky. The menu features sandwiches made on fresh homemade bread with all the best ingredients, a variety of pizza's served on Tandoori Naan bread or whole wheat pita, three to four soups made daily, a full coffee and espresso bar with the best lattes in town, desserts, ten craft beers on tap and an excellent wine selection. Along with the great food, Lizzie B's offers an unbelievable atmosphere that must be experienced to be appreciated. It's quickly becoming a favorite among locals and they always welcome new faces.

Monday – Wednesday:
10:00 am to 10:00 pm
Thursday – Saturday:
10:00 am to 11:30 pm

McGuire's Brickhouse

358 South Central Avenue
Prestonsburg KY 41653
606-886-0909
www.facebook.com/McGuiresBrickhouse

Built in 1917, this house-turned-restaurant was fully restored to take a step back in time. It is complete with a gold Victorian-style ceiling, rich mahogany wood, and even a sliding bookcase that makes this Prohibition-era house easily convert to the style of a speakeasy, hiding the added-on dining and bar areas. The large back patio and front deck make this a go-to spot on a warm day to enjoy your meal with friends outside. The food is one of a kind for the area. Dough for the pizza is made fresh daily to make it

a memorable experience. The favorite of locals thus far has been the unique Philly Cheesesteak Pizza. Burgers follow suit with unique toppings, such as the one that has the town's namesake mixed in—the 'Prestonsburger'.

You will find the recipe for this burger on the adjoining page, but you have to stop in to try the original.

Tuesday – Thursday: 11:00 am to 9:30 pm
Friday & Saturday: 11:00 am to 11:00 pm

The 'Prestonsburger'

8 ounces short rib Angus beef

**1 teaspoon House Seasoning
(or salt, pepper and your favorite
savory seasoning)**

Butter

Fresh baked kaiser bun

1 (1-ounce) slice Cheddar cheese

**2 slices applewood smoked bacon,
cooked**

**2 tablespoons (1 ounce) barbecue
sauce (we make ours with bourbon
and molasses but use your favorite
that has a kick)**

**⅓ cup (2½ ounces) fried onion
straws (French's French Fried Onions
would do)**

**2 tablespoons (1 ounce) brown
spicy mustard**

3 bread and butter pickles

Shape and pat beef to almost an inch thick. Season both sides of the patty and cook on a grill to medium well. Butter and toast buns when burger is close to done. While cooking burger, flip the patty a few times to get an even cook. (Do not press the burger. When you do, it sounds nice and sizzles but you lose a lot of juice and flavor.) When burger reaches the desired temperature, place cheese on top to melt it. It's time to build your burger. From the bottom up, start with bottom bun, then patty with cheese. Make an X with bacon, then top with barbecue sauce and onion straws. Spread mustard over top bun then top with pickles. Now, close it up and ENJOY. (Or better yet, come to McGuire's Brickhouse and have the original.) Don't worry; it's supposed to be messy.

Restaurant Recipe

THINKSTOCK/ISTOCK/WAYMOREAWESOMERCOLLECTION

Riverbend Pub & Grill

**229 Main Street
Vanceburg, KY 41179
606-796-3361
www.facebook.com/
riverbendvanceburg**

Riverbend Pub & Grill is a quaint little restaurant nestled on the Ohio River. The nautical-themed decor is pleasant and inviting to all who walk through the door. Riverbend offers a full breakfast, daily lunch and dinner specials, and desserts, along with pub appetizers and ice cold beverages. The food is always fresh, is prepared from scratch, and tastes great.

**Monday – Thursday: 7:00 am to 10:00 pm
Friday & Saturday: 7:30 am to 1:00 am**

Warm Potato Salad

My customers call and request this.

**5 russet potatoes, peeled and cubed
½ red onion, chopped
¼ cup minced fresh chives
½ red bell pepper, chopped
½ green bell pepper, chopped
½ celery stalk, finely chopped
6 bacon slices, cooked crisp and crumbled
½ cup mayo
1 to 2 tablespoons Dijon mustard
Dash sugar
Hot sauce
Salt
Pepper**

Cook and drain potatoes. Place in a large bowl; add onion, chives, peppers, celery and bacon. In separate bowl, combine mayonnaise and Dijon; add a dash each of sugar and hot sauce. Add to potato mixture and mix well. Season to taste with salt and pepper. Serve warm or cold.

Restaurant Recipe

Hard Cinnamon Candy

3¾ cups sugar

1½ cups white corn syrup

1 cup cold water

1 ounce cinnamon oil

Red food coloring

Combine sugar, syrup and water in a saucepan; stir together until sugar dissolves. Place over medium heat. Using a candy thermometer, cook until hard ball stage (250° to 265°). Remove from heat and add cinnamon oil and red food coloring to desired color—less for a lighter red, more for a darker red. Stir together. Pour onto a greased cookie sheet; cool. Break into pieces.

Variations: Use any flavoring and any coloring you like or to match the current holiday.

Restaurant Recipe

Golden Girls Parkway Restaurant

3749 Highway 15
Whitesburg, KY 41858
606-633-4680

Visit Golden Girls Parkway Restaurant for the best breakfast—served all day—that you have ever eaten. From biscuits and gravy to catfish and fried cornbread to Soup Bean Pie, Golden Girls is sure to please everyone who walks through their door. Where lots of love and hugs abound, you'll be a stranger only once and after that, you are family. While there, be sure and sign the guest book because owner Karen and the girls love to read about you. Enjoy fudge cakes and hard cinnamon candy that is made on site, and view art work by local artists. Golden Girls caters—nothing is too big or small. RVs are welcome with plenty of parking room.

Monday – Saturday: 7:00 am to 7:00 pm
Sunday: 7:00 am to 5:00 pm

THINKSTOCK/ ISTOCK/ VESNA CVOROVIC

Strawberry Fig Jam

3 cups mashed figs

3 cups sugar

2 (3-ounce) boxes strawberry Jell-O

Add all ingredients to a stock pot over medium-high heat. Cook, stirring very frequently, until boiling. A light foam may form across the top. There is no need to skim it off; just keep cooking and stirring. Continue to cook the liquid begins to shine, about 20 to 25 minutes.

As jam is cooking, place jar lids in a pan of hot, but not quite boiling, water. Run very hot water from the tap into the jars. (Repeat this again, just before filling jars; this heats the jars so they don't break when filling with hot jam.) Fill jars within ¼-inch of the top with hot jam. Wipe the rim of the jar clean to ensure a good seal. Put the lid (removed from hot water and used immediately) and rings on jar and tighten.

Place jars in boiling water to cover by 2 inches. Process in boiling water bath about 5 minutes. Carefully remove jars and place upside down on a towel. Once cooled, they're ready to store. Jam will keep up to 12 months.

Local Favorite

Appalachian Stack Cake

½ cup all-vegetable shortening

½ cup sugar

½ cup buttermilk

⅓ cup molasses

1 egg, slightly beaten

1 teaspoon vanilla extract

3½ cups all-purpose flour

½ teaspoon baking soda

½ teaspoon salt

½ teaspoon ground cinnamon

Pinch nutmeg

Powdered sugar for dusting

Preheat oven to 350°. Spray 6 (9-inch) cake pans with nonstick cooking spray. Line with parchment paper (cut into a circle), and spray parchment paper with cooking spray. Using an electric mixer, beat shortening and sugar until creamy. Add buttermilk, molasses, egg and vanilla, beating well. Add flour, baking soda, salt, cinnamon and nutmeg; mixing just until fully incorporated.

Remove dough to a lightly floured surface. Divided into 6 equal portions, patting each into a cake pan. Bake 10 to 12 minutes or until lightly browned. Remove from pans and cool completely on wire racks.

Apple Butter Filling:

4 cups chopped dried apples

1⅓ cup firmly packed dark brown sugar

1 teaspoon ground cinnamon

6 cups apple cider

In large saucepan, combine dried fruit, sugar and spices. Add enough cider to cover. Bring to a low boil and cook, stirring often, for 45 minutes. Cool 10 minutes, then use a blender or food processor to purée the mixture until smooth (adding additional cider only if needed).

While filling is still warm, spread between cake layers, stacking each on top as you go. Cover and refrigerate 24 hours before serving (if you can wait that long). Dust with powdered sugar just before serving.

Local Favorite

THINKSTOCK/ ISTOCK/ PHOTOSBYANDY

Index of Restaurants

Index of Restaurants

Index of Restaurants

Index of Recipes

    (continued on next page)

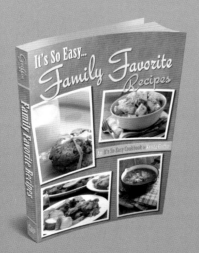

State Hometown Cookbook Series

A Hometown Taste of America, One State at a Time

EACH: $18.95 • 240 to 272 pages • 8x9 • paperbound • full color

Georgia
978-1-934817-01-8

Louisiana
978-1-934817-07-0

Mississippi
978-1-934817-08-7

South Carolina
978-1-934817-10-0

Tennessee
978-0-9779053-2-4

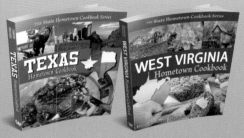

Texas
978-1-934817-04-9

West Virginia
978-1-934817-20-9

Each state's hometown charm is revealed through local recipes from real hometown cooks along with stories and photos that will take you back to your hometown... or take you on a journey to explore other hometowns across the country.

• Easy to follow recipes produce great-tasting dishes every time.
• Recipes use ingredients you already have in your pantry.
• Fun-to-read sidebars feature food-related festivals.
• The perfect gift or souvenir for anyone who loves to cook.

Eat & Explore Cookbook Series

Discover community celebrations and unique destinations, as they share their favorite recipes.

EACH: $18.95 • 240 to 272 pages • 7x9 • paperbound • full color

Arkansas
978-1-934817-09-4

Minnesota
978-1-934817-15-5

North Carolina
978-1-934817-18-6

Oklahoma
978-1-934817-11-7

Virginia
978-1-934817-12-4

Washington
978-1-934817-16-2

Collect them all. Call us toll-free **1.888.854.5954** *to order or to join our Cookbook Club.*

www.GreatAmericanPublishers.com • www.facebook.com/GreatAmericanPublishers

State Back Road Restaurants Series

From two-lane highways and interstates, to dirt roads and quaint downtowns, every road leads to delicious food when traveling across our United States. The STATE BACK ROAD RESTAURANTS COOKBOOK SERIES serves up a well-researched and charming guide to each state's best back road restaurants. No time to travel? No problem. Each restaurant shares with you their favorite recipes—sometimes their signature dish, sometimes a family favorite, but always delicious.

EACH: $18.95 • 256 pages • 7x9 • paperbound • full-color

  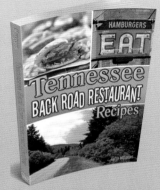

Alabama
978-1-934817-13-1

Kentucky
978-1-934817-17-9

Tennessee
978-1-934817-21-6

Don't miss out on our upcoming titles—join our Cookbook Club and you'll be notified of each new edition.

www.GreatAmericanPublishers.com • www.facebook.com/GreatAmericanPublishers

---

ORDER FORM

Mail to: Great American Publishers • 171 Lone Pine Church Road • Lena, MS 39094
Or call us toll-free 1.888.854.5954 to order by check or credit card.

❑ Check Enclosed

Charge to: ❑ Visa ❑ MC ❑ AmEx ❑ Disc

Card# _____

Exp Date _____

Signature _____

Name _____

Address _____

City _____ State _____ Zip _____

Phone _____

Email _____

QTY.	TITLE	TOTAL
___	_____	_____
___	_____	_____
___	_____	_____
___	_____	_____
___	_____	_____
___	_____	_____
	Subtotal	_____
	Postage ($3 first book; $.50 each additional)	_____
	Total	_____